James Russell Lowell

Lectures on English Poets

James Russell Lowell

Lectures on English Poets

ISBN/EAN: 9783337777876

Printed in Europe, USA, Canada, Australia, Japan

Cover: Foto ©Thomas Meinert / pixelio.de

More available books at **www.hansebooks.com**

LECTURES ON ENGLISH POETS

BY
JAMES RUSSELL LOWELL

"—CALL UP HIM WHO LEFT HALF-TOLD
THE STORY OF CAMBUSCAN BOLD."

CLEVELAND
THE ROWFANT CLUB
MDCCCXCVII

CONTENTS

		PAGE
INTRODUCTION, .		vii
LECTURE I, DEFINITIONS, . . .		3
LECTURE II, PIERS PLOUGHMAN'S VISION,		23
LECTURE III, THE METRICAL ROMANCES, . . .		39
LECTURE IV, THE BALLADS, . . .		59
LECTURE V, CHAUCER, . .		79
LECTURE VI, SPENSER, ...		97
LECTURE VII, MILTON, . .		117
LECTURE VIII, BUTLER, ...		135
LECTURE IX, POPE, .		149
LECTURE X, POETIC DICTION, . .		167
LECTURE XI, WORDSWORTH, . .		183
LECTURE XII, THE FUNCTION OF THE POET, .		199

INTRODUCTION

WHILST midway in his thirty-fifth year Lowell was appointed to deliver a course of lectures before the Institute founded by a relative, and bearing the family name. He was then known as the author of two volumes of poems besides the biting "Fable for Critics" and the tender "Vision of Sir Launfal," and the nimbus was still brightly shining around the head of him who had created the tuneful "Hosea Biglow" and the erudite "Parson Wilbur." It was not the accident of relationship that procured this appointment; he had fairly earned the honor by his scholarly acquirements and poetly achievements.

When the twelfth and last lecture had been delivered, the correspondent of the "New York Evening Post" wrote:

"Mr. Lowell has completed his course of lectures on English Poetry, which have been attended

INTRODUCTION

throughout by crowded audiences of the highest intelligence. The verdict of his hearers has been a unanimous one of approval and delight. Certainly no course of literary lectures has ever been delivered here so overflowing with vigorous, serious thought, with sound criticism, noble, manly sentiments, and genuine poetry. Mr. Lowell is a poet, and how could a true poet speak otherwise?

"His appointment to the Professorship of Belles Lettres in Harvard College, made vacant by the resignation of Longfellow, is the very best that could have been made, and gives high satisfaction. It is such names that are a tower of strength and a crown of glory to our Alma Mater. Everett, Sparks, Ticknor, Longfellow, Agassiz, Peirce, are known in their respective departments wherever science and polite letters have a foothold, and the nomination of James Russell Lowell as the associate and successor of such men is the most 'fit to be made.'"

A quarter of a century after their delivery, one who heard them bore this testimony: "The lectures made a deep impression upon cultivated auditors, and full reports of them were printed in the Boston 'Advertiser.' Their success was due to their intrinsic merits. The popular lecturer is often led to imitate the vehement action of the stump-speaker and the drollery of the comedian by turns. Mr. Lowell's pronunciation is clear and precise, and the modulations of his voice unstudied and agreeable, but he seldom if ever raised a hand for gesticulation, and his voice was kept in its natural compass. He read like one who had something of importance to utter, and the just emphasis was felt in the penetrating tone. There were no oratorical climaxes, and no pitfalls set for applause. But the weighty thoughts, the earnest feeling, and the brilliant poetical images gave to every discourse an indescribable charm. The younger portion of the audience, especially, enjoyed a feast for which all the study of their lives had been a preparation."

The same auditor, writing after Lowell's death, mentions them again: "In 1854 [it was really 1855] Lowell delivered a course of twelve lectures on the British Poets at the Lowell Institute. They were not printed at the time, except, partially, in newspaper reports, but doubtless many of their ideas were absorbed in the published essays. In these lectures the qualities of his prose style began to be manifested. It was felt by every hearer to be the prose of a poet, as it teemed with original images, fortunate epithets, and artistically wrought allusions, and had a movement and music all its

INTRODUCTION

own. A few friends from Cambridge attended these lectures, walking into the city, and more than once through deep snow. The lecturer humorously acknowledged his indebtedness to them, saying that when he saw their faces he was in the presence of his literary conscience. These lectures have not been published as yet, and may not be."

Even while they were yet ringing in the ears of those delighted audiences, Ticknor and Fields were eager to publish them, but Lowell withheld consent. The lectures had been rapidly written, and needed the labor of the file, and this the unexpected duties of the equally unexpected professorship precluded. There were five applicants for the chair vacated by Longfellow, but Lowell was not one of them; both his nomination and his appointment were made without his knowledge. He accepted the chair with the understanding that he should be allowed to spend one year abroad for some necessary study in Germany and Spain. Then his professorial duties engaged him and the "Lectures on English Poets" were left as a waif stranded on the forgotten columns of a newspaper. When at length the opportunity of leisure came Lowell found himself capable

INTRODUCTION

of better things, and he was satisfied with absorbing into later essays some fragments of the early lectures. There ended his concern for them; but an enthusiastic hearer had preserved the Boston "Advertiser's" reports of them in a special scrap-book, which ultimately became the property of the University of Michigan and thus fell into the editor's hands, who felt the charm thereof, and was desirous of sharing his pleasure with the *Rowfant Club*.

There is little doubt that Lowell had been too fastidious when he wrote to James T. Fields, in May, 1855: " It has just got through my skull, and made a dint into my sensorium, that you wrote me a note, ever so long ago, about my lectures and the publication of them. I don't mean to print them yet — nor ever till they are better — but, at any rate, I consider myself one of your flock, though not, perhaps, as lanigerous as some of them." And when Lowell's literary executor wrote: " His powers of critical appreciation and reflection were displayed to advantage in these lectures. No such discourses had been heard in America. They added greatly to his reputation as critic, scholar, and poet," — there could be no hesitation in setting aside Lowell's modest self-depreciation. After the delivery of his first lecture, he had written to his friend Stillman: "So far as the public are concerned, I have succeeded." And his words are as true in 1896 as they were in 1855; and although his literary art was not so consummate as it became in his ultimate development, these early lectures will aid and encourage the student by showing his growth: we see the rivulet become the flowing river.

We share, too, in the delight of his first audience on reading:

"The lines of Dante seem to answer his every mood: sometimes they have the compressed implacability of his lips, sometimes they ring like an angry gauntlet thrown down in defiance, and sometimes they soften or tremble as if that stern nature would let its depth of pity show itself only in a quiver of the voice."

"So in 'Paradise Lost' not only is there the pomp of long passages that move with the stately glitter of Milton's own angelic squadrons, but if you meet anywhere a single verse, that, too, is obstinately epic, and you recognize it by its march as certainly as you know a friend by his walk."

"Who can doubt the innate charm of rhyme whose eye has ever been delighted by the visible consonance of a tree growing at once toward an upward and a downward heaven, on the edge of the unrippled river; or as the kingfisher flits from shore to shore, his silent echo flies under him and completes the vanishing couplet in the visionary world below."

"Every desire of the heart finds its gratification in the poet because he always speaks imaginatively and satisfies ideal hungers."

And see, too, how the "powers of critical appreciation" that Professor Norton has mentioned were bursting into blossom and giving promise of the golden harvest to come:

"Sir Thomas Browne, * * * a man who gives proof of more imagination than any other Englishman except Shakspeare."

For subtlety and depth of insight Lowell has never excelled this early example, nor has he ever outdone the critical estimate, so true and so terse, of his final pronouncement upon Pope:

"Measured by any high standard of imagination, he will be found wanting; tried by any test of wit, he is unrivaled."

And what of such a shining felicity as where he meets Sir Thomas Browne on common ground and the author of "Religio Medici" gravely smiles and acknowledges kinship:

"If a naturalist showed us a toad we should feel indifferent, but if he told us that it had been found in a block of granite we should instantly look with profound interest on a creature that perhaps ate moths in Abel's garden or hopped out of the path of Lamech."

Most truly "No such lectures had been heard in America," and as truly they deserve to be made more than a delightful memory for the early hearers alone.

Lowell wrote to a friend that at his first lecture he had held his audience for an hour and a quarter, but the reporter's notes of that lecture fall far short of that fullness; nevertheless, compared with Anstey's shorthand notes of Carlyle's lectures on the "History of Literature," we come much nearer to the living voice in the Boston "Advertiser's" reports of these Lowell lectures. Carlyle spoke without a written text, nor had he any notes save a few bits of paper which in his hyper-nervousness he twisted out of all hope of reportorial decipherment— and without once looking at them; Lowell had his

INTRODUCTION

manuscripts (written *currente calamo*, for the new wine of life was in full ferment and it was no small feat to bottle any of it successfully), and we are assured from internal evidence that the "Advertiser's" reporter was allowed access to them. His text has a *tang* as characteristic as Thoreau's wild apples, and we do not feel the dubiety of the blind patriarch, "The voice is Jacob's, but the hands are Esau's." No; it is James Russell Lowell, his voice, his inimitable mark, and these are his words sounding in our ears after half a century.

The only attempt at "editing" has been as far as possible to reproduce the reporter's "copy." To that end Lowell's profusion of capitals is retained (and the reader will bear in mind that the Transcendental spirit was then in both the air and the alphabet), and even his italics, suggested, as Mr. Underwood says, by the speaker's emphasis, find their respective places. Here and there a compositor's error has been corrected and a proof-reader's oversight adjusted; sometimes this has been conjectural, and again the needful change was obvious. In all else, save the applause, this Rowfant Book may be called a faint echo of the Lowell Institute Lectures.

INTRODUCTION

It is "printed, but not published" in loving fealty to Lowell's memory, and every Rowfanter has at heart the assurance that his Shade will look upon this literary *flotsam* without a frown, or with one that will soon fade into forgiveness.

S. A. J.

ANN ARBOR, November 10th, 1896.

LECTURE I

DEFINITIONS

(Tuesday Evening, January 9, 1855)

I

MR. LOWELL began by expressing his sense of the responsibility he had assumed in undertaking a course of lectures on English Poets. Few men, he said, had in them twelve hours of talk that would be worth hearing on *any* subject; but on a subject like poetry no person could hope to combine in himself the qualities that would enable him to do justice to his theme. A lecturer on science has only to show how much he knows — the lecturer on Poetry can only be sure how much he *feels*.

Almost everybody has a fixed opinion about the merits of certain poets which he does not like to have disturbed. There are no fanaticisms so ardent as those of Taste, especially in this country, where we are so accustomed to settle everything by vote that if a majority should decide to put a stop to the precession of the Equinoxes we should expect to hear no more of that interesting ceremony.

A distinguished woman [Mrs. Stowe] who has lately published a volume of travels, affirms that it is as easy to judge of painting as of poetry by instinct. It *is* as easy. But without reverent study of their works no instinct is competent to judge of the masters of either art.

Yet every one has a right to his private opinion, and the critic should deal tenderly with illusions which give men innocent pleasure. You may sometime see japonicas carved out of turnips, and if a near-sighted friend should exclaim, "What a pretty japonica!" do not growl "Turnip!" unless, on discovering his mistake, he endeavors to prove that the imitation is as good as the real flower.

In whatever I shall say, continued Mr. Lowell, I shall, at least, have done my best to think before I speak, making no attempt to say anything new, for it is only strange things and not new ones that come by effort. In looking up among the starry poets I have no hope of discovering a new Kepler's law — one must leave such things to great mathematicians like Peirce. I shall be content with resolving a nebula or so, and bringing to notice some rarer shade of color in a double star. In our day a lecturer can hardly hope to instruct. The press has so diffused intelligence that everybody has just misinformation enough on every subject to make him thoroughly uncomfortable at the misinformation of everybody else.

Mr. Lowell then gave a brief outline of his course,

stating that this first lecture would indicate his point of view, and treat in part of the imaginative faculty.

After some remarks upon Dr. Johnson's "Lives of the Poets," the lecturer proceeded: Any true criticism of poetry must start from the axiom that what distinguishes that which we call the poetical in anything, and makes it so, is that it transcends the understanding, by however little or much, and is interpreted by the intuitive operation of some quite other faculty of the mind. It is precisely the something-more of feeling, of insight, of thought, of expression which for the moment lulls that hunger for the superfluous which is the strongest appetite we have, and which always gives the lie to the proverb that enough is as good as a feast. The boys in the street express it justly when they define the indefinable merit of something which pleases them, by saying it is a touch beyond — or it is first-rate and a half. The poetry of a thing is this touch beyond, this third half on the farther side of first-rate.

Dr. Johnson said that that only was good poetry out of which good prose could be made. But poetry cannot be translated into prose at all. Its condensed meaning may be paraphrased, and you get the sense of it, but lose the condensation which is a part of its essence. If on Christmas day you should give your son a half-eagle, and should presently take it back, and give him the excellent prose version of five hundred copper cents, the boy would doubtless feel that the translation had precisely the same meaning in tops, balls, and gibraltars; but the feeling of infinite riches in a little room, of being able to carry in his waistcoat pocket what Dr. Johnson would have called the potentiality of tops and balls and gibraltars beyond the dreams of avarice — this would have evaporated. By *good* prose the Doctor meant prose that was sensible and had a meaning. But he forgot his own theory sometimes when he thought he was writing poetry. How would he contrive to make any kind of sense of what he says of Shakspeare? that

> Panting Time toiled after him in vain.

The difference between prose and poetry is one of essence and not one of accident. What may be called the negatively poetical exists everywhere. The life of almost every man, however prosaic to himself, is full of these dumb melodies to his neighbor. The farmer looks from the hillside and sees the tall ship lean forward with its desire for the ocean, every full-hearted sail yearning seaward, and takes passage with her from his drudgery to the beautiful conjectured land. Meanwhile he himself has Pegasus yoked to his plough without knowing it, and the sailor, looking back, sees him sowing his field with the graceful idyl of summer and harvest. Little did the needle-woman dream that she was stitching passion and pathos into her weary seam, till Hood came and found them there.

The poetical element may find expression either in prose or verse. The "Undine" of Fouqué is poetical, but it is not poetry. A prose writer may have imagination and fancy in abundance and yet not be a poet. What is it, then, that peculiarly distinguishes the poet? It is not merely a sense of the beautiful, but so much keener *joy* in the sense of it (arising from a greater fineness of organization) that the emotion must *sing*, instead of only *speaking* itself.

The first great distinction of poetry is *form* or arrangement. This is not confined to poems alone, but is found involved with the expression of the poetical in all the Arts. It is here that the statue bids good-bye to anatomy and passes beyond it into the region of beauty; that the painter passes out of the copyist and becomes the Artist.

Mr. Lowell here quoted Spenser's statement of Plato's doctrine:

> For of the soul the body form doth take,
> For soul is form and doth the body make.

This coördination of the spirit and form of a poem is especially remarkable in the "Divina Commedia" of Dante and the "Paradise Lost" of Milton, and that not only in the general structure, but in particular parts. The lines of Dante seem to answer his every mood: sometimes they have the compressed implacability of his lips, sometimes they ring like an angry gauntlet thrown down in defiance, and sometimes they soften or tremble as if that stern nature would let its depth of pity show itself only in a quiver of the voice; but always and everywhere there is subordination, and the pulse of the measure seems to keep time to the footfall of the poet along his fated path, as if a fate were on the verses too. And so in the "Paradise Lost" not only is there the pomp of long passages that move with the stately glitter of Milton's own angelic squadrons, but if you meet anywhere a single verse, that, too, is obstinately epic, and you recognize it by its march as certainly as you know a friend by his walk.

The instinctive sensitiveness to order and proportion, this natural incapability of the formless and vague, seems not only natural to the highest poetic genius, but to be essential to the universality and permanence of its influence over the minds of men. The presence of it makes the charm of Pope's

"Rape of the Lock" perennial; its absence will always prevent such poems as the "Faëry Queene," "Hudibras," and the "Excursion" (however full of beauty, vivacity, and depth of thought) from being popular.

Voltaire has said that epic poems were discourses which at first were written in verse only because it was not yet the custom to narrate in prose. But instead of believing that verse is an imperfect and undeveloped prose, it seems much more reasonable to conclude it the very consummation and fortunate blossom of speech, as the flower is the perfection towards which the leaf yearns and climbs, and in which it at last attains to fullness of beauty, of honey, of perfume, and the power of reproduction.

There is some organic law of expression which, as it must have dictated the first formation of language, must also to a certain extent govern and modulate its use. That there is such a law a common drum-head will teach us, for if you cover it with fine sand and strike it, the particles will arrange themselves in a certain regular order in sympathy with its vibrations. So it is well known that the wood of a violin shows an equal sensibility, and an old instrument is better than a new one because all resistance has been overcome. I have observed, too, as something that distinguishes singing birds from birds of prey, that their flight is made up of a series of parabolic curves, with rests at regular intervals, produced by a momentary folding of the wings; as if the law of their being were in some sort metrical and they *flew* musically.

Who can doubt the innate charm of rhyme whose eye has ever been delighted by the visible consonance of the tree growing at once toward an upward and a downward heaven on the edge of an unrippled river; or, as the kingfisher flits from shore to shore, his silent echo flies under him and completes the vanishing couplet in the visionary world below? Who can question the divine validity of number, proportion, and harmony, who has studied the various rhythms of the forest? Look for example at the pine, how its branches, balancing each other, ray out from the tapering stem in stanza after stanza, how spray answers to spray, and leaf to leaf in ordered strophe and antistrophe, till the perfect tree stands an embodied ode, through which the unthinking wind cannot wander without finding the melody that is in it and passing away in music.

Language, as the poets use it, is something more than an expedient for conveying thought. If mere meaning were all, then would the Dictionary be always the most valuable work in any tongue, for in it exist potentially all eloquence, all wisdom, all pathos, and all wit. It is a great wild continent of words ready to be tamed and subjugated, to have its meanings and uses applied. The prose writer finds there his quarry and his timber; but the poet enters it like Orpheus, and makes its wild inmates sing and dance and keep joyous time to every wavering fancy of his lyre.

All language is dead invention, and our conversational currency is one of shells like that of some African tribes—shells in which poetic thoughts once housed themselves, and colored with the tints of morning. But the poet can give back to them their energy and freshness; can conjure symbolic powers out of the carnal and the trite. For it is only an enchanted sleep, a simulated death, that benumbs language; and see how, when the true prince-poet comes, the arrested blood and life are set free again by the touch of his fiery lips, and as Beauty awakens through all her many-chambered palace runs a thrill as of creation, giving voice and motion and intelligence to what but now were dumb and stiffened images.

The true reception of whatever is poetical or imaginative presupposes a more exalted, or, at least, excited, condition of mind both in the poet and the reader. To take an example from daily life, look at the wholly diverse emotions with which a partizan and an indifferent person read the same political newspaper. The one thinks the editor a very sound and moderate person whose opinion is worth having on a practical question; the other wonders to see one very respectable citizen drawn as a Jupiter Tonans, with as near an approach to real thunderbolts as printer's ink and paper will concede, and another, equally respectable and a member of the same church, painted entirely black, with horns, hoofs, and tail. The partizan is in the receptive condition just spoken of; the indifferent occupies the solid ground of the common sense.

To illustrate the superiority of the poetic imagination over the prosaic understanding, Mr. Lowell quoted a story told by Le Grand in a note to one of his "Fabliaux." A sinner lies dying, and an angel and a fiend, after disputing the right to his soul, agree to settle the affair by a throw of dice. The fiend gets the first chance, and the fatal cubes come up — two sixes! He chuckles and rubs his claws, for everybody knows that no higher number is possible. But the angel thinks otherwise, throws, and, behold, a six and seven! And thus it is, that when the understanding has done its best, when it has reached, as it thinks, down to the last secret of music and meaning that language is capable of, the poetical sense comes in with its careless mir-

DEFINITIONS

acle, and gets one more point than there are in the dice.

Imagination is not necessarily concerned with poetic expression. Nothing can be more poetical than the lines of Henry More the Platonist:

> What doth move
> The nightingale to sing so fresh and clear?
> The thrush or lark, that mounting high above,
> Chants her shrill notes to heedless ears of corn,
> Heavily hanging in the dewy morn.

But compare it with Keats'

> Ruth, when sick for home,
> She stood in tears amid the *alien* corn.

The imagination has touched that word "alien," and in it we see the field through Ruth's eyes, as *she* looked round on the hostile spikes, and not through those of the poet.

Imagination enters more or less into the composition of all *great* minds, all minds that have what we call *breadth* as distinguished from mere force or acuteness. We find it in philosophers like Plato and Bacon, in discoverers like Kepler and Newton, in fanatics like George Fox, and in reformers like Luther.

The shape which the imaginative faculty will take

is modified by the force of the other qualities with which it is coördinated in the mind. If the moral sense predominates, the man becomes a reformer, or a fanatic, and his imagination gets itself uttered in his life. Bunyan would have been nothing but a fanatic, if he had not been luckily shut up in Bedford jail, alone with his imagination, which, unable to find vent in any other way, possessed and tortured him till it had wrung the "Pilgrim's Progress" out of him—a book the nearest to a poem, without being one, that ever was written. Uniting itself with the sense of form, Imagination makes a sculptor; with those of form and color, a painter; with those of time and tune, a musician. For in itself it is dumb, and can find expression only through the help of some other faculty.

Imagination *plus* the poetic sense is poesy, *minus* the poetic sense it is science, though it may clothe itself in verse. To those who are familiar with Dr. Donne's verses, I need only mention his name as a proof of my last position. He solves problems in rhyme, that is all.

Shakspeare was so charged with the highest form of the poetic imagination, as some persons are with electricity, that he could not point his finger at a word without a spark of it going out of him. I will illustrate it by an example taken at random from him. When Romeo is parting from Juliet, Shakspeare first projects his own mind into Romeo, and then, as Romeo becomes so possessed with the emotion of the moment that his words take color from it, all nature is infected and is full of *partings*. He says:

> But look what *curious* streaks
> Do lace the *severing* clouds.

Shakspeare's one hundred and thirteenth sonnet was here also quoted in illustration.

The highest form of imagination, Mr. Lowell said, is the dramatic, of which Shakspeare must always stand for the only definition. Next is the narrative imagination, where the poet forces his own personal consciousness upon us and makes our senses the slaves of his own. Of this kind Dante's "Divina Commedia" is the type. Below this are the poems in which the imagination is more diffused; where the impression we receive is rather from *mass* than from particulars; where single lines are not so strong in themselves as in forming integral portions of great sweeps of verse; where effects are produced by allusion and suggestion, by sonorousness, by the use of names which have a traditional poetic value. Of this kind Milton is the type.

Lastly, said Mr. Lowell, I would place in a class by themselves those poets who have properly no imagination at all, but only a pictorial power. These we may call the imaginary poets, writers who give us images of things that neither they nor we believe in or can be deceived by, like pictures from a magic lantern. Of this kind are the Oriental poems of Southey, which show a knowledge of Asiatic mythologies, but are not livingly mythologic.

Where the imagination is found in combination with great acuteness of intellect, we have its secondary or prose form. Lord Bacon is an example of it. Sir Thomas Browne is a still more remarkable one — a man who gives proof of more imagination than any other Englishman except Shakspeare.

Fancy is a frailer quality than Imagination, and cannot breathe the difficult air of the higher regions of intuition. In combination with Sentiment it produces poetry; with Experience, wit. The poetical faculty is in closer affinity with Imagination; the poetical temperament with Fancy. Contrast Milton with Herrick or Moore. In illustration Mr. Lowell quoted from Marvell, the poet of all others whose fancy hints always at something beyond itself, and whose wit seems to have been fed on the strong meat of humor.

As regards *man*, Fancy takes delight in life, manners, and the result of culture, in what may be called *Scenery;* Imagination is that mysterious something which we call Nature — the unfathomed base on which Scenery rests and is sustained. Fancy deals with feeling; Imagination with passion. I have sometimes thought that Shakspeare, in the scene of the "Tempest," intended to typify the isle of *Man,* and in the characters, some of the leading qualities or passions which dwell in it. It is not hard to find the Imagination in Prospero, the Fancy in Ariel, and the Understanding in Caliban; and, as he himself was the poetic imagination incarnated, is it considering too nicely to think that there is a profound personal allusion in the breaking of Prospero's wand and the burying of his book to the nature of that man who, after such thaumaturgy, could go down to Stratford and live there for years, only collecting his dividends from the Globe Theatre, lending money on mortgage, and leaning over the gate to chat and chaffer with his neighbors?

I think that every man is conscious at times that it is only his borders, his seaboard, that is civilized and subdued. Behind that narrow strip stretches the untamed domain, shaggy, unexplored, of the natural instincts. Is not this so? Then we can narrow our definition yet farther, and say that Fancy and Wit appear to the artificial man; Imagination and Humor to the natural man. Thus each of us in his dual capacity can at once like Chaucer and Pope, Butler and Jean Paul, and bury the hatchet of one war of tastes.

And now, finally, what is the secret of the great poet's power over us? There is something we love better than love, something that is sweeter to us than riches, something that is more inspiring to us than success—and that is the imagination of them. No woman was ever loved enough, no miser was ever rich enough, no ambitious man ever successful enough, but in imagination. Every desire of the heart finds its gratification in the poet because he speaks always imaginatively and satisfies ideal hungers. We are the always-welcome guests of his ennobling words.

This, then, is why the poet has always been held in reverence among men. All nature is dumb, and we men have mostly but a stunted and stuttering speech. But the longing of every created thing is for utterance and expression. The Poet's office, whether we call him Seer, Prophet, Maker, or Namer, is always this—to be the Voice of this lower world. Through him, man and nature find at last a tongue by which they can utter themselves and speak to each other. The beauties of the visible world, the trembling attractions of the invisible, the hopes and desires of the heart, the aspirations of the soul, the passions and the charities of men; nay, the trees, the rocks, our poor old speechless mother, the earth herself, become voice and music, and attain to that humanity, a divine instinct of which is implanted in them all.

LECTURE II

PIERS PLOUGHMAN'S VISION

(*Friday Evening, January 12, 1855*)

II

IN literature, as in religion and politics, there is a class of men who may be called Fore-runners. As there were brave men before Agamemnon, so there must have been brave poets before Homer. All of us, the great as well as the little, are the result of the entire Past. It is but just that we should remember now and then that the very dust in the beaten highways of thought is that of perhaps nameless saints and heroes who thought and suffered and died to make commonplace practicable to us. Men went to the scaffold or the stake for ideas and principles which we set up in our writings and our talk as thoughtlessly as a printer sticks his type, and the country editor, when he wrote his last diatribe on the freedom of the press, dipped his pen without knowing it in the blood of the martyrs. It would be well for us to remember, now and then, our dusty benefactors, and to be conscious that we are under bonds to the Present to the precise amount that we are indebted to the Past.

Thus, from one point of view, there is nothing

more saddening than a biographical dictionary. It is like a graveyard of might-have-beens and used-to-be's, of fames that never ripened and of fames already decayed. Here lies the great Thinker who stammered and could not find the best word for his best thought, and so the fame went to some other who had the gift of tongues. Here lies the gatherer of great masses of learning from which another was to distil the essence, and to get his name upon all the phials and show-bills. But if these neglected headstones preach the vanity of a selfish ambition, they teach also the better lesson that every man's activity belongs not to himself but to his kind, and whether he will or not must serve at last some other, greater man. We are all foot-soldiers, and it is out of the blood of a whole army of us that iron enough is extracted to make the commemorative sword that is voted to the great Captain.

In that long aqueduct which brings the water of life down to us from its far sources in the Past, though many have done honest day-labor in building it, yet the keystone that unites the arch of every period is engraved with the name of the greatest man alone. These are our landmarks, and mentally we measure by these rather than by any scheme of Chronology. If we think of Philosophy, we think of four or five great names, and so of Poetry, Astronomy, and the rest. Geology may give what age she will to the globe; it matters not, it will still be only so many great men old; and wanting these, it is in vain that Egypt and Assyria show us their long bead-roll of vacant centuries. It is in the life of its great men that the life and thought of a people becomes statuesque, rises into poetry, and makes itself sound out clearly in rhythm and harmony.

These great persons get all the fame and all the monuments like the generals of armies, though *we* may lead the forlorn hope, or make a palpitating bridge with our bodies in the trenches. Rank and file may grumble a little — but it is always so, and always must be so. Fame would not be fame if it were or could be divided infinitesimally, and every man get his drachm and scruple. It is good for nothing unless it come in a lump. And besides, if every man got a monument or an epitaph who felt quite sure he deserved it, would marble hold out, or Latin?

The fame of a great poet is made up of the sum of all the appreciations of many succeeding generations, each of which he touches at some one point. He is like a New World into which explorer after explorer enters, one to botanize, one to geologize, one to ethnologize, and each bringing back his report.

His great snowy mountains perhaps only one man in a century goes to the top of and comes back to tell us how he saw from them at once the two great oceans of Life and Death, the Atlantic out of which we came, the Pacific toward which we tend.

Of the poet we do not ask everything, but the best expression of the *best* of everything. If a man attain this but once, though only in a frail song, he is immortal; while every one who falls just short of it, if only by a hair's breadth, is as sure to be forgotten. There is a wonderful secret that poets have not yet learned, and this is that small men cannot do great things, but that the small man who can do small things *best* is great. The most fatal ill-success is to almost succeed, as, in Italy, the worst lemons are those large ones which come nearest to being oranges. The secret of permanent fame is to express some idea the most compactly, whether in your life, your deed, or your writing. I think that if anything is clear in history, it is that every idea, whether in morals, politics, or art, which is laboring to express itself, feels of many men and throws them aside before it finds the one in whom it can incarnate itself. The noble idea of the Papacy (for it *was* a noble one — nothing less than the attempt to embody the higher law in a human institution) whispered itself to many before it got the man it wanted in Gregory the Great. And Protestantism carried numbers to the stake ere it entered into Luther: a man whom nature made on purpose — all asbestos so that he could not burn. Doubtless Apollo spoiled many a reed before he found one that would do to pipe through even to the sheep of Admetus, and the land of song is scattered thick with reeds which the Muse has experimented with and thrown away.

It is from such a one that I am going to try to draw a few notes of music and of mirth to-night. Contemporary with Chaucer lived a man who satirized the clergy and gave some lively pictures of manners before the "Canterbury Tales" were written. His poem was very popular, as appears from the number of manuscript copies of it remaining, and after being forgotten for two centuries, it was revived again, printed, widely read, and helped onward the Reformation in England. It has been reprinted twice during the present century. This assures us that it must have had a good deal of original force and vivacity. It may be considered, however, to be tolerably defunct now. This poem is the vision of Piers Ploughman.

I have no hope of reviving it. Dead poets are something *very* dead, and critics blow their trumpets over them in vain. What I think is interesting and instructive in the poem is that it illustrates in a remarkable manner what may be considered the Anglo-Saxon element in English poetry. I refer to race, and not to language. We find here a vigorous common-sense, a simple and hearty love of nature, a certain homely tenderness, held in check always by a dogged veracity. Instead of Fancy we have Feeling; and, what more especially deserves notice, there is almost an entire want of that sense of form and outline and proportion which alone brings anything within the province of Art. Imagination shows itself now and then in little gleams and flashes, but always in the form of Humor. For the basis of the Anglo-Saxon mind is beef and beer; what it considers the *real* as distinguished from, or rather opposed to, the *ideal*. It spares nothing merely because it is beautiful. It is the Anglo-Saxon who invented the word *Humbug*, the potent exorcism which lays the spirit of poetry in the Red Sea. It is he who always translates Shows into Shams.

Properly speaking, "Piers Ploughman's Vision" is not a poem at all. It is a sermon rather, for no verse, the chief end of which is not the representation of the beautiful, and whose moral is not included in that, can be called poetry in the true sense of the word. A thought will become poetical by being put into verse when a horse hair will turn into a snake by being laid in water. The poetical nature will delight in Mary Magdalen more for her fine hair than for her penitence. But whatever *is* poetical in this book seems to me characteristically Saxon. The English Muse has mixed blood in her veins, and I think that what she gets from the Saxon is a certain something homely and practical, a flavor of the goodwife which is hereditary. She is the descendant on one side of Poor Richard, inspired, it is true, but who always brings her knitting in her pocket. The light of the soul that shines through her countenance, that "light that never was on land or sea," is mingled with the warm glow from the fireside on the hearth of Home. Indeed, may it not be attributed to the Teutonic heart as something peculiar to it, that it has breadth enough to embrace at once the chimney-corner and the far-reaching splendors of Heaven? Happy for it when the smoke and cookery-steam of the one do not obscure the other!

I find no fault with the author of Piers Ploughman for not being a poet. Every man cannot be a poet (fortunately), nor every poet a great one. It is the privilege of the great to be always contemporaneous, to speak of fugacious events in words that shall be perennial. But to the poets of the second rate we go for pictures of manners that have passed away, for transitory facts, for modes of life and ways of thinking that were circumstantial merely. They give us reflections of our outward, as their larger brethren do of our inward, selves. They deal, as it were, with costume; the other with man himself.

But these details are of interest, so fond are we of facts. We all have seen the congregation which grew sleepy while the preacher talked of the other world give a stir of pleased attention if he brought in a personal anecdote about *this*. Books are written and printed, and we read them to tell us how our forefathers cocked their hats, or turned up the points of their shoes; when blacking and starch were introduced; who among the Anglo-Saxons carried the first umbrella, and who borrowed it.

These trifles, also, acquire importance in proportion as they are older. If a naturalist showed us a toad, we should be indifferent, but if he told us that it had been found in a block of granite, we should instantly look with profound interest on a creature that perhaps ate moths in Abel's garden, or hopped out of the path of Lamech. And the same precious jewel of instruction we find in the ugly little facts embedded in early literatures. They teach us the unchangeableness of man and his real independence of his accidents. He is the same old lay figure under all his draperies, and sits to one artist for a John and to another for a Judas, and serves equally well for both portraits. The oldest fable reappears in the newest novel. Aristophanes makes coats that fit us still. Voltaire is Lucian translated into the eighteenth century. Augustus turns up in Louis Napoleon. The whirligig of Time brings back at regular intervals the same actors and situations, and under whatever names — Ormuzd and Ahriman, Protestantism and Catholicism, Reform and Conservatism, Transcendentalism and Realism. We see the same ancient quarrel renewed from generation to generation, till we begin to doubt whether this be truly the steps of a Tower of Babel that we are mounting, and not rather a treadmill, where we get all the positive good of the exercise and none of the theoretic ill which might come if we could once solve the problem of getting above ourselves. Man's life continues to be, as the Saxon noble described it, the flight of a sparrow through a lighted hall, out of one darkness and into another, and the two questions *whence?* and *whither?* were no tougher to Adam than to us. The author of Piers Ploughman's Vision has offered us his theory of this world and the next, and in doing so gives some curious hints of modes of life and of thought. It is generally agreed that one of his names was Langland, and it is disputed whether the other was Robert or William. Robert has the most authority, and William the strongest arguments in its favor. It is of little consequence now to him or us. He was probably a monk at Malvern. His poem is a long one, written in the unrhymed alliterative measure of the Anglo-Saxon poetry, and the plan of it is of the simplest kind. It is a continued allegory, in which all the vices, passions, and follies of the time, the powers of the mind, the qualities of the spirit, and the theological dogmas of the author, are personified and mixed up with real personages with so much simplicity, and with such unconscious interfusion of actual life as to give the whole an air of probability.

The author of Piers Ploughman's Vision avoids any appearance of incongruity by laying his scene in a world which is neither wholly real nor wholly imaginary — the realm of sleep and dreams. There it does not astonish us that Langland should meet and talk with the theological virtues, and that very avoirdupois knights, monks, abbots, friars, and ploughmen should be found in company with such questionable characters as Do-well, Do-better, Do-best, Conscience, Nature, Clergy, and Activa Vita. He has divided his poem into twenty "steps," as he calls them, in each of which he falls asleep, has a dream, and wakes up when it becomes convenient or he is at a loss what else to do. Meanwhile his real characters are so very real, and his allegorical ones mingle with them on such a common ground of easy familiarity, that we forget the allegory altogether. We are not surprised to find those Utopian edifices, the Tower of Truth and the Church of Unity, in the same street with an alehouse as genuine as that of Tam o' Shanter, and it would seem nothing out of the common if we should see the twelve signs of the Zodiac saving themselves from Deucalion's flood in an arc of the Ecliptic.

Mr. Lowell here read long extracts from the poem, with a commentary of his own, generally brief, of which we can give only the following fine passage on Personification.

The truth is, that ideal personifications are commonly little better than pinchbeck substitutes for imagination. They are a refuge which unimaginative minds seek from their own sterile imaginativeness. They stand in the same relation to poetry as wax figures to sculpture. The more nearly they counterfeit reality, the more unpleasant they are, and there is always a dejected irresponsibleness about the legs and a Brattle street air in the boots that is ludicrous. The imagination gives us no pictures, but the thing itself. It goes out for the moment to dwell in and inform with its own life the object of its vision — as Keats says somewhere in one of his letters, "I hop about the gravel and pick up crumbs in the sparrows." And so, in personifying, the imagination must have energy to project its own emotion so as to see it objectively — just as the disease of the hypochondriac runs before him in a black dog. Thus it was that the early poets, "who believed the wonders that they sang," peopled the forests, floods, and mountains with real shapes of beauty or terror; and accordingly in primitive times *ecstasy* is always attributed to the condition of the poetic mind. To the great poets these ecstasies are still possible, and personification had its origin in the tradition of these, and the endeavor of inferior minds to atone for their own languor by what we may call historical or reminiscental imagination. Here is indicated the decline from faith to ritual. Shakspeare has illustrated the true secret of imaginative personification when he makes the conscience of Macbeth become external and visible to him in the ghastly shape at the banquet which he alone can see, and Lady Macbeth's afterwards in the blood-stain on her hand. This is the personification of the creative mind whose thoughts are not images, but *things*. And this seems to have been the normal condition of Shakspeare's genius, as it is the exceptional one of all other poets. He alone has embodied in flesh and blood his every thought and fancy and emotion, his every passion and temptation. Beside him all other poets seem but the painters and not the makers of men. He sent out his profound intellect to look at life from every point of view, and through the eyes of all men and women from the highest to the lowest. In every one he seems to have tapped it with the knuckles, to have said sadly, *Tinnit, inane est,* It rings, it is hollow; and then to have gone down quietly to wait for death and another world at Stratford.

As fine an example as any of the prose imagination, of the intellect acting pictorially, is where Hobbes compares the Papacy to the ghost of the Roman Empire sitting upon its tomb. This implies a foregone personification, but the pleasure it gives springs chiefly from our sense of its historic and intellectual truth. And this subordinate form of imagination uses typically and metaphorically those forms in which ecstasy had formerly visibly clothed itself, flesh-and-blooded itself, so to speak; as where Lord Bacon says that Persecution in the name of Religion is "to bring down the Holy Ghost, not in the likeness of a dove, but in the shape of a vulture or a raven."

After reading more extracts from the poem, Mr. Lowell concluded his lecture in these words:

Truly it seems to me that I can feel a heart beat all through this old poem, a manly, trustful, and tender one. There are some men who have what may be called a vindictive love of Truth — whose love of it, indeed, seems to be only another form of hatred to their neighbor. They put crooked pins on the stool of repentance before they invite the erring to sit down on it. Our brother Langland is plainly not one of these.

What I especially find to our purpose in Piers Ploughman, as I said before, is that it defines with tolerable exactness those impulses which our poetry has received from the Anglo-Saxon as distinguished from the Anglo-Norman element of our race. It is a common Yankee proverb that there is a great deal of human nature in man. I think it especially true of the Anglo-Saxon man. We find in this poem common sense, tenderness, a love of spiritual goodness without much sensibility to the merely beautiful, a kind of *domestic* feeling of nature and a respect for what is established. But what is still more noticeable is that man is recognized as man, and that the conservatism of Langland is predicated upon the well-being of the people.

It is impossible to revive a dead poem, but it is pleasant, at least, to throw a memorial flower upon its grave.

LECTURE III

THE METRICAL ROMANCES

(Tuesday Evening, January 16, 1855)

III

WHERE is the Golden Age? It is fifty years ago to every man and woman of three-score and ten. I do not doubt that aged Adam babbled of the superiority of the good old times, and, forgetful in his enthusiasm of that fatal bite which set the teeth of all his descendants on edge, told, with a regretful sigh, how much larger and finer the apples of his youth were than that to which the great-grandson on his knee was giving a preliminary polish. Meanwhile the great-grandson sees the good times far in front, a galaxy of golden pippins whereof he shall pluck and eat as many as he likes without question. Thus it is that none of us knows when Time is with him, but the old man sees only his shoulders and that inexorable wallet in which youth and beauty and strength are borne away as alms for Oblivion; and the boy beholds but the glowing face and the hands stretched out full of gifts like those of a St. Nicholas. Thus there is never any present good; but the juggler, Life, smilingly baffles us all, making us believe that the vanished ring is under his left hand or his right, the past or the future, and shows us at last that it was in our own pocket all the while.

So we may always listen with composure when we hear of Golden Ages passed away. Burke pronounced the funeral oration of one — of the age of Chivalry — the period of Metrical Romances — of which I propose to speak to-night. Mr. Ruskin — himself as true a knight-errant as ever sat in a demipique saddle, ready to break a lance with all comers, and resolved that even the windmills and the drovers shall not go about their business till they have done homage to his Dulcinea — for the time being joins in the lament. Nay, what do we learn from the old romances themselves, but that all the heroes were already dead and buried? Their song also is a threnody, if we listen rightly. For when did Oliver and Roland live? When Arthur and Tristem and Lancelot and Caradoc Break-arm? In that Golden Age of Chivalry which is always past.

Undoubtedly there was a great deal in the institution of Chivalry that was picturesque; but it is noticeable in countries where society is still picturesque that dirt and ignorance and tyranny have the chief hand in making them so. Mr. Fenimore Cooper thought the American savage picturesque, but if he had lived in a time when it was necessary that one should take out a policy of insurance on his scalp or wig before going to bed, he might have seen them in a different light. The tourist looks up with delight at the eagle sliding in smooth-winged circles on the icy mountain air, and sparkling back the low morning sun like a belated star. But what does the lamb think of him? Let us look at Chivalry a moment from the lamb's point of view.

It is true that the investiture of the Knight was a religious ceremony, but this was due to the Church, which in an age of brute force always maintained the traditions at least of the intellect and conscience. The vows which the Knights took had as little force as those of god-parents, who fulfil their spiritual relation by sending a piece of plate to the god-child. They stood by each other when it was for their interest to do so, but the only virtue they had any respect for was an arm stronger than their own. It is hard to say which they preferred to break — a head, or one of the Ten Commandments. They looked upon the rich Jew with thirty-two sound teeth in his head as a providential contrivance, and practised upon him a comprehensive kind of dental surgery, at once for profit and amusement, and then put into some chapel a painted window with a Jewish prophet in it for piety — as if *they* were the Jewish profits they cared about. They outraged and robbed their vassals in every conceivable manner, and, if *very* religious, made restitution on their death-beds by giving a part of the plunder (when they could keep it no longer) to have masses sung for the health of their souls — thus contriving, as they thought, to be their own heirs in the other world. Individual examples of heroism are not wanting to show that man is always paramount to the institutions of his own contriving, so that any institution will yield itself to the compelling charms of a noble nature. But even were this not so, yet Sir Philip Sidney, the standard type of the chivalrous, grew up under other influences. So did Lord Herbert of Cherbury, so did the incomparable Bayard; and the single fact that is related as a wonderful thing of Bayard, that, after the storming of Brescia, he respected the honor of the daughter of a lady in whose house he was quartered, notwithstanding she was beautiful and in his power, is of more weight than all the romances in Don Quixote's library.

But what form is that which rises before us, with features in which the gentle and forgiving reproach of the woman is lost in the aspiring power of the martyr?

THE METRICAL ROMANCES

We know her as she was,

> The whitest lily in the shield of France,
> With heart of virgin gold,

that bravest and most loyal heart over whose beatings knightly armor was ever buckled, that saintly shape in which even battle looks lovely, that life so pure, so inspired, so humble, which stands there forever to show us how near womanhood ever is to heroism, and that the human heart is true to an eternal instinct when it paints Faith and Hope and Charity and Religion with the countenances of women.

We are told that the sentiment of respect for woman, a sentiment always remarkable in the Teutonic race, is an inheritance from the Institution of Chivalry. But womanhood must be dressed in silk and miniver that chivalry may recognize it. That priceless pearl hidden in the coarse kirtle of the peasant-girl of Domremy it trampled under its knightly feet — shall I say? — or swinish hoofs. Poor Joan! The chivalry of France sold her; the chivalry of England subjected her to outrages whose burning shame cooled the martyr-fire, and the King whom she had saved, the very top of French Knighthood, was toying with Agnes Sorel while the fagots were crackling around the savior of himself and his kingdom in the square of Rouen!

Thank God, that our unchivalric generation can hack the golden spurs from such recreant heels! A statue stands now where her ashes were gathered to be cast into the Seine, but her fittest monument is the little fountain beneath it, the emblem of her innocence, of her inspiration, drawn not from court, or castle, or cloister, but from the inscrutable depths of that old human nature and that heaven common to us all—an emblem, no less, that the memory of a devoted life is a spring where all coming times may drink the holy waters of gratitude and aspiration. I confess that I cannot see clearly that later scaffold in the Place de la Révolution, through the smoke of this martyr-fire at Rouen, but it seems to me that, compared with this *woman*, the Marie Antoinette, for whose sake Burke lamented the downfall of chivalry, is only the daughter of a king.

But those old days, whether good or bad, have left behind them a great body of literature, of which even yet a large part remains unprinted. To this literature belong the Metrical Romances. Astonished by the fancy and invention so abundantly displayed by the writers of these poems, those who have written upon the subject have set themselves gravely to work to find out what country they could have got them from. Mr. Warton, following Dr.

Warburton, inclines to assign them to an Oriental origin. Dr. Percy, on the other hand, asserts a Scandinavian origin; while Ritson, who would have found it reason enough to think that the sun rose in the West if Warton or Percy had taken the other side, is positive that they were wholly French. Perhaps the truth lies somewhere between the positions of Percy and Ritson. The Norman race, neither French nor Scandinavian, was a product of the mingled blood of both, and in its mental characteristics we find the gaiety and lively fancy of the one tempering what is wild in the energy and gloomy in the imagination of the other.

We know the exact date of the arrival of the first Metrical Romance in England. Taillefer, a Norman minstrel, brought it over in his head, and rode in the front at the battle of Hastings singing the song of Roland. Taillefer answers precisely the description of a Danish skald, but he sang in French, and the hero he celebrated was one of the peers of Charlemagne, who was himself a German.

> Taillefer, who well could sing a strain,
> Upon a swift horse rode amain
> Before the Duke and chanted loud
> Of Charlemagne and Roland good,
> Of Oliver and vassals brave
> Who found at Roncesvalles their grave.

What this song of Roland was it is impossible to say, as the only copy of it seems to have perished with Taillefer at the battle of Hastings; but it was probably of the same kind with many of those which have survived and brought down to us the exploits of Arthur and his knights.

With regard to a large part of the romances of the Round Table, and those which grew out of them, it is tolerably certain that, although written in French, they were made in England.

One of the great charms of the Metrical Romances is the innocent simplicity with which they commit anachronisms. Perhaps it would be more exact to call them synchronisms, for, with the most undoubting faith, they compel all other times to adopt the dress, manners, and conventionalities of their own. To them there was no one world, nor ever had been any, except that of Romance. They conferred retrospective knighthood upon the patriarchs; upon Job, David, and Solomon. Joseph of Arimathea became Sir Joseph of that ilk. Even the soldier who pierced the side of Jesus upon the cross was made into Sir Longinus and represented as running a tilt with our Lord. All the heroes of the Grecian legend were treated in the same way. They translated the old time and the old faith into new, and thus completed the outfit of their own imaginary world, supplying it at a very cheap rate with a Past and with mythology. And as they believed the gods and genii of the Pagan ancients to have been evil spirits who, though undeified, were imperishable in their essence, they were allowed to emigrate in a body from the old religion into the new, where they continued to exercise their functions, sometimes under their former names, but oftener in some disguise. These unfortunate aliens seem to have lived very much from hand to mouth, and after the invention of holy water (more terrible to them than Greek-fire) they must have had rather an uncomfortable time of it. The giants were received with enthusiasm, and admitted to rights of citizenship in the land of Romance, where they were allowed to hold fiefs and castles in consideration of their eminent usefulness in abducting damsels, and their serving as anvils to the knights, who sometimes belabored them for three days at a time, the fight ending at last, not from failure of breath on the part of the combatants but of the minstrel. As soon as *he* has enough, or sees that his hearers have, the head of the unhappy giant becomes loose on his shoulders.

Another charm of the romances is their entire inconsequentiality. As soon as we enter this wonderful country the old fetters of cause and effect drop from our limbs, and we are no longer bound to give a reason for anything. All things come to pass in that most charming of ways which children explain by the comprehensive metaphysical formula—" 'cause." Nothing seems to be premeditated, but a knight falls in love, or out of it, fights, goes on board enchanted vessels that carry him to countries laid down on no chart, and all without asking a question. In truth, it is a delightful kind of impromptu life, such as we all should like to lead if we could, with nothing set down in the bills beforehand.

But the most singular peculiarity of Romance-land remains to be noticed—there are no *people* in it, that is, no common people. The lowest rank in life is that of a dwarf. It is true that if a knight loses his way there will always be a clown or two to set him right. But they disappear at once, and seem to be wholly phantasmagoric, or, at best, an expedient rendered necessary by the absence of guide-posts, and the inability of the cavaliers to read them if there had been any. There are plenty of Saracens no doubt, but they are more like cucumbers than men, and are introduced merely that the knight may have the pleasure of slicing them.

We cannot claim any condensed poetical merit for the Metrical Romances. They have very few quotable passages and fewer vigorous single lines. Their merit consists in a diffuse picturesqueness, and reading them is like turning over illuminated missals in a traveler's half-hour, which leave a vague impression on the mind of something vivid and fanciful, without one's being able to recall any particular beauty. Some of them have great narrative merit, being straightforward and to the purpose, never entangling themselves in reflection or subordinating the story to the expression. In this respect they are refreshing after reading many poems of the modern school, which, under the pretense of sensuousness, are truly sensual, and deal quite as much with the upholstery as with the soul of poetry. The thought has nowadays become of less importance than the vehicle of it, and amid the pomp of words we are too often reminded of an Egyptian procession, in which all the painful musical instruments then invented, priests, soldiers, and royalty itself, accompany the triumphal chariot containing perhaps, after all, only an embalmed monkey or a pickled ibis.

There is none of this nonsense in the Old Romances, though sometimes they are tediously sentimental, and we wonder as much at the capacity of our ancestors in bearing dry verses as dry blows. Generally, however, they show an unaffected piety and love of nature. The delight of the old minstrels in the return of Spring is particularly agreeable, and another argument in favor of the Northern origin of this class of poems. Many of them open with passages like this:

> Merry it is in the month of May,
> When the small fowls sing their lay,
> Then flowers the apple-tree and perry,
> And the little birds sing merry;
> Then the ladies strew their bowers
> With red roses and lily flowers,
> The damisels lead down the dance,
> And the knights play with shield and lance.

Some of the comparisons, also, drawn from Nature, are as fresh as dew. For example, when a lady sees her lover:

> She is as glad at that sight
> As the birds are of the light.

Or,

> As glad as grass is of the rain.

A knight is said to be

> As weary as water in a weir,

a simile full of imagination.

The most airy glimpses of the picturesque occur sometimes; as describing a troop of knights:

> They rode away full serriedly,
> Their gilded pennons of silk of Ind
> Merrily rattled with the wind;
> The steeds so noble and so wight
> Leaped and neighed beneath each knight.

After quoting various specimens of these poems, Mr. Lowell gave the following sketch of the manners and customs of Romance-land, "condensed from the best authorities."

If you are born in this remarkable country and destined for a hero, the chances are that by the time you are seven years old your father will have gone off to fight the infidels, and a neighboring earl will have taken possession of his estates and his too-hastily-supposed widow. You resent this in various ways, especially by calling your stepfather all the proper names you can think of that are improper. He, for some unexplained reason, is unable to get rid of you, though he tries a variety of plots level with the meanest capacity. You, being of uncommon sagacity, are saved by the aid of three or four superfluous miracles. Meanwhile you contrive to pick up a good knightly education, and by the time you are seventeen are bigger and stronger and handsomer than anybody else, except, of course, the giants. So, one day you buckle on your armor, mount your horse, who is as remarkable in his way as yourself, and go adventuring. Presently you come to a castle where you are most courteously received. Maidens as white as whale's bone and fair as flowers (they are all so in Romance-land) help you off with your armor, and dress you in richest silks. You then go to dine with the Lord of the Castle, who is a knight of very affable manners and agreeable conversation, but with an aversion to religious topics. His daughter, the fairest lady on the ground, assists at the meal. You are conducted to your chamber, and after a refreshing sleep meet your host and hostess at breakfast. At a suitable time you return thanks for your kind treatment and ask for your horse. The knight, however, in the blandest manner tells you that a little custom of his will interfere with your departure. He is in the habit of fighting with all his guests, and has hitherto been successful in killing them all to the number of several hundred. This is precisely the account which you are fond of settling, and after a few allusions to Mahomed and Termagant and Alcoban, you accept the challenge and, of course, come off victor. This seems to settle the matter for the young lady whom your lance has just promoted to her inheritance, and she immediately offers herself and her estates to you, telling you, at the same time, that she had long been secretly a Christian. Though madly in love with her, and interested in her religious views, which she details to you at some length, you mount your steed and ride away, but without being expected to give any reasons. You have a particular mission nowhere, and on your way to that interesting country you kill a *megalosaurus* (for whose skeleton Professor Owen would have given his ears), and two or three incidental giants. Riding on, you come to a Paynim-land, ruled over by a liberally-minded Soldan, who receives you into favor after you have slain some thousands of his subjects to get an appetite for dinner. The Soldan, of course, has a daughter, who is converted by you, and, of course, offers you her hand. This makes you think of the other lady, and you diplomatize. But there is another Paynim-land, and another Soldan, who sends word that he intends to marry your beautiful convert.

The embassy of the proud Paynim somehow results in your being imprisoned for seven years, when it suddenly occurs to you that you might as well step out. So you pick up a magic sword that has been shut up with you, knock down the jailers, mount your horse which is waiting at the door, and ride off. Now, or at some other convenient time, you take occasion to go mad for a year or two on account of ladye-love number one. But hearing that ladye-love number two is about to yield to the addresses of her royal suitor, who has killed her father, burned his capital, and put all his subjects to the sword, you make some appropriate theological disquisitions and start to the rescue. On your way you meet a strange knight, join combat with him without any questions on either side, and after a doubtful fight of a day or two, are mutually overcome with amazement at finding anybody who cannot be beaten. Of course it turns out that the strange knight is your father; you join forces, make short work with the amorous Soldan and his giants, and find yourself encumbered with a young lady, a princess too, all of whose relatives and vassals have been slaughtered on your account, and who naturally expects you to share her throne. In a moment of abstraction you consent to the arrangement, and are married by an archbishop *in partibus* who happens to be on the spot. As your late royal rival has slain all your late father-in-law's lieges, and you have done the same service for him in turn, there are no adventures left in this part of the world. Luckily, before the wedding-ring is warm on your finger, a *plesiosaurus* turns up. This saves many disagreeable explanations with the bride, whom you are resolved to have nothing to do with while the other young lady is alive. You settle her comfortably on the throne of her depopulated kingdom, slay the monster, and start for home with your revered parent. There you overcome the usurping Earl, reinstate your father, and assist cheerfully at the burning of your mother for bigamy; your filial piety being less strong than your reverence for the laws of your country. A fairy who has a particular interest in you (and who, it seems, is your real mother, after all — a fact which relieves your mind of any regrets on the score of the late melancholy bonfire), lets you into the secret that ladye-love the first is your own sister. This revives your affection for your wife, and you go back to the kingdom of Gombraunt, find her reduced to extremities by another matrimonial Soldan, whom you incontinently massacre with all *his* giants, and now at last a prospect of quiet domestic life seems to open. Dull, peaceful days follow, and you begin to take desponding views of life, when your *ennui* is pleasantly broken in upon by a monster who combines in himself all the monstrosities of heraldic zoölogy. You decapitate him and incautiously put one of his teeth in your boot as a keepsake. A scratch ensues, physicians are in vain, and you die with an edifying piety, deeply regretted by your subjects, if there are any left with their heads on.

On the whole, we may think ourselves happy that we live under somewhat different institutions.

LECTURE IV

THE BALLADS

(*Friday Evening, January* 19, 1855)

IV

ONE of the laws of the historical Macbeth declares that "Fools, minstrels, bards, and all other such idle people, unless they be specially licensed by the King, shall be compelled to seek some craft to win their living," and the old chronicler adds approvingly, "These and such-like laws were used by King Macbeth, through which he governed the realm ten years in good justice."

I do not quote this in order to blacken the memory of that unhappy monarch. The poets commonly contrive to be even with their enemies in the end, and Shakspeare has taken an ample revenge. I cite it only for the phrase *unless they be specially licensed by the King*, which points to a fact on which I propose to dwell for a few moments before entering upon my more immediate object.

When Virgil said, "Arma virumque cano," "Arms and the man I sing," he defined in the strictest manner the original office of the poet, and the object of the judicious Macbeth's ordinance was to prevent any one from singing the wrong arms and the rival man. Formerly the poet held a recognized place in the body politic, and if he has been deposed from it, it may be some consolation to think that the *Fools,* whom the Scottish usurper included in his penal statute, have not lost their share in the government of the world yet, nor, if we may trust appearances, are likely to for some time to come. But the Fools here referred to were not those who had least, but those who had most wit, and who assumed that disguise in order to take away any dangerous appearance of intention from their jibes and satires.

The poet was once what the political newspaper is now, and circulated from ear to ear with satire or panegyric. He it was who first made public opinion a power in the State by condensing it into a song. The invention of printing, by weakening the faculty of memory, and by transferring the address of language from the ear to the eye, has lessened the immediate power of the poet. A newspaper may be suppressed, an editor may be silenced, every copy of an obnoxious book may be destroyed, but in those old days when the minstrels were a power, a verse could wander safely from heart to heart and from hamlet to hamlet as unassailable as the memories on which it was imprinted.

THE BALLADS

Its force was in its impersonality, for public opinion is disenchanted the moment it is individualized, and is terrible only so long as it is the opinion of no one in particular. Find its author, and the huge shadow which but now darkened half the heaven shrinks like the genius of the Arabian story into the compass of a leaden casket which one can hold in his hand. Nowadays one knows the editor, perhaps, and so is on friendly terms with public opinion. You may have dined with it yesterday, rubbed shoulders with it in the omnibus to-day, nay, carried it in your pocket embodied in the letter of the special correspondent.

Spenser, in his prose tract upon Ireland, has left perhaps the best description possible of the primitive poet as he was everywhere when the copies of a poem were so many living men, and all publication was to the accompaniment of music. He says: "There is amongst the Irish a certain kind of people called bards, which are to them instead of poets, whose profession is to set forth the praises or dispraises of men in their poems or rhythms; the which are held in such high regard or esteem amongst them that none dare to displease them for fear of running into reproach through this offense, and to be made infamous in the mouths of all men."

Nor was the sphere of the bards confined to the

present alone. They were also the embodied memory of the people. It was on the wings of verse that the names of ancestral heroes could float down securely over broad tracts of desert time and across the gulfs of oblivion. And poets were sometimes made use of by sagacious rulers to make legends serve a political purpose. The Persian poet Firdusi is a remarkable instance of this. Virgil also attempted to braid together the raveled ends of Roman and Greek tradition, and it is not impossible that the minstrels of the Norman metrical romances were guided by a similar instinct.

But the position of the inhabitants of England was a peculiar one. The Saxons by their conversion to Christianity, and the Normans still more by their conversion and change of language, were almost wholly cut off from the past. The few fragments of the Celtic race were the only natives of Britain who had an antiquity. The English properly so called were a people who hardly knew their own grandfathers. They no longer spoke the language, believed in the religion, or were dominated by the ideas of their ancestors.

English writers demand of us a national literature. But where for thirteen centuries was their own? Our ancestors brought a past with them to Plymouth; they claimed descent from a great race;

the language they spoke had been ennobled by recording the triumphs of ancestral daring and genius; it had gone up to Heaven wafted on the red wings of martyr-fires; mothers hushed their new-born babes, and priests scattered the farewell earth upon the coffin-lid, with words made sweet or sacred by immemorial association. But the Normans when they landed in England were a new race of armed men almost as much cut off from the influences of the past as those which sprang out of the ground at the sowing of the dragon's teeth. They found there a Saxon encampment occupying a country strange to them also. For we must remember that though Britain was historically old, England was not; and it was as impossible to piece the histories of the two together to make a national record of as it would be for us to persuade ourselves into a feeling of continental antiquity by adopting the Mexican annals.

The ballads are the first truly national poetry in our language, and national poetry is not either that of the drawing-room or of the kitchen. It is the common mother-earth of the universal sentiment that the foot of the poet must touch, through which shall steal up to heart and brain that fine virtue which puts him in sympathy, not with his class, but with his kind.

Fortunately for the ballad-makers, they were not encumbered with any useless information. They had not wit enough to lose their way. It is only the greatest brains and the most intense imagination that can fuse learning into one substance with their own thought and feeling, and so interpenetrate it with *themselves* that the acquired is as much *they* as the native. The ballad-makers had not far to seek for material. The shipwreck, the runaway match, the unhappy marriage, the village ghost, the achievement of the border outlaw — in short, what we read every day under the head of *Items* in the newspapers, were the inspiration of their song. And they sang well, because they thought, and felt, and believed just as their hearers did, and because they never thought anything about it. The ballads are pathetic because the poet did not try to make them so; and they are models of nervous and simple diction because the business of the poet was to *tell* his story, and not to adorn it; and accordingly he went earnestly and straightforwardly to work, and let the rapid thought snatch the word as it ran, feeling quite sure of its getting the right one. The only art of expression is to have something to express. We feel as wide a difference between what is manufactured and what is spontaneous as between the sparkles of an electrical machine, which a sufficiently muscular professor can grind out by the dozen, and the wildfire of God that writes *mene, mene,* on the crumbling palace walls of midnight cloud.

It seems to me that the ballad-maker, in respect of diction, had also this advantage—that he had no books. Language, when it speaks to the eye only, loses half its meaning. For the eye is an outpost of the brain, and wears its livery oftener than that of the character. But the temperament, the deep human nature, the aboriginal emotions, *these* utter themselves in the voice. It is only by the ear that the true mother-tongue that knows the short way to the heart is learned. I do not believe that a man born deaf could understand Shakspeare, or sound anything but the edges and shores of Lear's tempestuous woe. I think that the great masters of speech have hunted men and not libraries, and have found the secret of their power in the street and not upon the shelf.

It is the *way* of saying things that is learned by commerce with men, and the best writers have mixed much with the world. It is there only that the language of feeling can be acquired.

The ballads are models of narrative poetry. They are not concerned with the utterance of thought, but only of sentiment or passion, and it is as illustrating poetic diction that I shall chiefly cite them. If they moralize it is always by picture, and not by preachment. What discourse of inconstancy has the force and biting pathos of this grim old song, the "Twa Corbies"?

> As I was walking all alone
> I heard twa corbies making a moan.
> The one unto the other did say:
> Where shall we gang and dine to-day?
> In beyond that old turf dyke
> I wot there lies a new-slain knight,
> And naebody kens that he lies there,
> But his hawk and his hound and his lady fair.
> His hound is to the hunting gone,
> His hawk to fetch the wild-fowl hame,
> His lady's ta'en anither mate —
> Sae we may make our dinner sweet.
> You'll sit upon his white neck-bone
> And I'll pick out his bonny blue een;
> With a lock of his golden hair
> We'll thatch our nest when it grows bare.
> Many a one for him makes moan,
> But none sall ken where he is gone;
> O'er his white bones when they grow bare
> The wind shall blow forever mair.

Observe, the wind simply blows. That is enough; but a modern poet would have sought to intensify by making the wind moan, or shriek, or sob, or something of the kind.

Mr. Lowell here quoted a ballad which tells a story of a child-murder. It begins:

> Fair Anne sate in her bower
>   Down by the greenwood side,
> And the flowers did spring,
> And the birds did sing,
>   'T was the pleasant Mayday tide.

The ballad singers had all the advantage of that spur of the moment which the excitement of speaking gives, and they also received the magnetism which came from the sympathy of their hearers. They knew what *told*, for they had their hand upon the living pulse of feeling. There was no time to palaver; they must come to the point.

> The Percy came out of Northumberland,
>   And a vow to God made he
> That he would hunt in the mountains
>   Of Cheviot within days three,
> In the maugre of Doughty Douglas
>   And all that ever with him be.

They plunge into deep water at once. And there is never any filling up. The transitions are abrupt. You can no more foretell the swift wheel of the feeling than that of a falcon, and the phrases flash forth sharp-edged and deadly like a sword drawn in wrath. The passions speak out savagely and without any delicacies of circumlocution.

It is worth thinking of whether the press, which we have a habit of calling such a fine institution, be not weakening the fibre and damaging the sincerity of our English and our thinking, quite as fast as it diffuses intelligence.

Consider the meaning of expression — something wrung from us by the grip of thought or passion, whether we will or no. But the editor is quite as often compelled to write that he may fill an empty column as that he may relieve an overfilled brain. And in a country like ours, where newspapers are the only reading of the mass of the people, there is a danger of a general contentedness in commonplace. For we always become what we habitually read. We let our newspapers think for us, argue for us, criticize for us, remember for us, do everything for us, in short, that will save us from the misfortune of being *ourselves*. And so, instead of men and women, we find ourselves in a world inhabited by incarnated leaders, or paragraphs, or items of this or that journal. We are apt to wonder at the scholarship of the men of two centuries ago. They were scholars because they did not read so much as we do. We spend more time over print than they did, but instead of communing with the choice thought of choice spirits, and insensibly acquiring the grand manner of that supreme society, we diligently inform ourselves of such facts as that a fine horse belonging to Mr. Smith ran away on Wednesday and that a son of Mr. Brown fell into the canal on Thursday, or that a gravel bank fell in and buried Patrick O'Callahan on Friday. And it is our own fault, and not that of the editor. For *we* make the newspapers, and the editor would be glad to give us better stuff if we did not *demand* such as this.

Another evil of this state of things is the watering, or milk-and-watering, of our English. Writing to which there is no higher compelling destiny than the coming of the printer's devil must end in this at last. The paragraphist must make his paragraph, and the longer he makes it, the better for him and the worse for us. The virtue of words becomes wholly a matter of length. Accordingly, we have now no longer any fires, but "disastrous conflagrations"; nobody dies, but "deceases" or "demises"; men do not fall from houses, but are "precipitated from mansions or edifices"; a convict is not hanged, but "suffers the extreme penalty of the offended law," etc.

The old ballad-makers lived in a better day.

They did not hear of so many events that none of them made any impression. They did not live, as we do, in a world that seems a great ear of Dionysius, where if a scandal is whispered in Pekin we hear of it in New York. The minstrels had no metaphysical bees in their bonnets. They did not speculate about this world or the next. They had not made the great modern discovery that a bird in a bush is worth two in the hand. They did not analyze and refine till nothing genuine was left of this beautiful world but an indigestion.

The ballads neither harangue nor describe; but only state things in the least complex way. Those old singers caught language fresh and with a flavor of the soil in it still, and their hearers were people of healthy sensibilities who must be hit directly and hard. Accordingly, there is a very vigorous handling. They speak bluntly and to the purpose. If a maiden loses her lover, she merely

> Turns her face unto the wall
> And there her heart it breaks.

A modern poet would have hardly thrown away the opportunity offered him for describing the chamber and its furniture; he would put a painted window into it — for the inkstand will supply them quite as cheaply as plain glass. He would tell you all about the tapestry which the eyes of the dying maiden in her extreme agony would have been likely, of course, to have been minutely interested in. He would have given a clinical lecture on the symptoms, and a post-mortem examination. It was so lucky for those old ballad-mongers that they had not any ideas! And when they give a dying speech they do not make their heroes take leave of the universe in general as if *that* were going into mourning for a death more or less.

When Earl Douglas is in his death-thraw, he says to his nephew:

> My wound is deep; I fain would sleep;
>   Take thou the vanguard of the three.
> And hide me by the brakenbush
>   That grows on yonder lily lee.
> O bury me by the brakenbush
>   Beneath the blooming brere.
> Let never living mortal ken
>   That a kindly Scot lies here.

The ballads are the only true folk-songs that we have in English. There is no other poetry in the language that addresses us so simply as mere men and women. Learning has tempered with modern poetry, and the Muse, like Portia, wears a doctor's cap and gown.

The force and earnestness of style that mark the old ballad become very striking when contrasted with later attempts in the same way. It is not flatness and insipidity that they are remarkable for, but for a bare rocky grandeur in whose crevices tenderness nestles its chance tufts of ferns and harebells. One of these sincere old verses imbedded in the insipidities of a modern imitation looks out stern and colossal as that charcoal head which Michael Angelo drew on the wall of the Farnesina glowers through the paling frescoes.

Mr. Lowell here read a number of passages from the old ballad entitled "Margaret's Ghost," and compared them with a few stanzas from an "improved" version of the same by Mallet. He also read from the ballad of "Helen of Kirkconnell," and from others.

Of the tenderness of the ballads I must give an instance or two before I leave them. In the old ballad of "Clerk Saunders," Margaret follows the ghost of her lover to his grave.

> So painfully she climbed the wall,
>   She climbed the wall up after him,
> Hose nor shoon upon her feet,
>   She had no time to put them on.

O bonny, bonny, sang the bird
   Sat on a coil o' hay,
But mournfu', mournfu', was the maid
   That followed the corpse o' clay.

Is there any room at your head, Saunders?
   Or any room at your feet?
Is there any room at your side, Saunders?
   For fain, fain I would sleep.

She's sat her down upon the grave
   And mourned sae lang and sair
That the clochs and wanton flies at last
   Came and built in her yellow hair.

In further illustration Mr. Lowell read from the "Clerk's Two Sons of Oxenford." He concluded his lecture thus:

I think that the makers of the old ballads did stand face to face with life in a way that is getting more and more impossible for us. Day by day the art of printing isolates us more and more from our fellows and from the healthy and inspiring touch of our fellows. We continually learn more and more of mankind and less of man. We know more of Europe than of our own village. We feel humanity from afar.

But I must not forget that the ballads have

passed through a sieve which no modern author has the advantage of. Only those have come down to us which imprinted themselves on the general heart. The new editions were struck off by mothers crooning their children to sleep, or by wandering minstrels who went about sowing the seeds of courtesy and valor in the cottage and on the hillside. Print, which, like the amber, preserves all an author's grubs, gives men the chance to try him by the average, rather than the best, of his yield.

Moreover, the Review of the ballad-singer was in the faces of his ring of hearers, in whose glow or chill he could read at a glance a criticism from which there was no appeal. It was not Smith or Brown, but the human heart that judged him.

Doubtless another advantage of these old poets was their out-of-door life. They went from audience to audience on foot, and had no more cramped a study than the arch of heaven, no library but clouds, streams, mountains, woods, and men. There is something more in sunshine than mere light and heat. I fancy that a kind of flavor we detect in the old ballads is due to it, and that it may give color and bloom to the brain as well as to the apple and plum. Indoor inspiration is like the stove-heat of the forcing-house, and the fruits ripened by it are pale, dropsical, and wanting in *tang*. There may be also a virtue in the fireside which gives to the Northern wind a domestic and family warmth, and makes it skilled to teach the ethics of home. But it is not to the chimney-corner that we can trace the spiritual dynasties that have swayed mankind. These have sunshine in their veins.

Perhaps another charm of these ballads is that nobody made them. They seem to have come up like violets, and we have only to thank God for them. And we imply a sort of fondness when we call them "old." It is an epithet we give endearingly and not as supposing any decrepitude or senescence in them. Like all true poetry, they are not only young themselves, but the renewers of youth in us; they do not lose, but accumulate, strength and life. A true poem gets a part of its inspiring force from each generation of men. The great stream of Homer rolls down to us out of the past, swollen with the tributary delight and admiration of the ages. The next generation will find Shakspeare fuller of meaning and energy by the addition of our enthusiasm. Sir Philip Sidney's admiration is part of the breath that sounds through the trumpet of "Chevy Chase." That is no empty gift with which we invest a poem when we bestow on it our own youth, and it is no small debt we owe the true poem that it preserves for us some youth to bestow.

LECTURE V

CHAUCER

(Tuesday Evening, January 23, 1855)

V

IT is always a piece of good fortune to be the earliest acknowledged poet of any country. We prize the first poems as we do snowdrops, not only for their own intrinsic beauty, but even more for that force of heart and instinct of sunshine in them which brings them up, where grass is brown and trees are bare, the outposts and forlorn hopes of spring. There never comes anything again like a *first* sensation, and those who love Chaucer, though they may have learned late to do it, cannot help imaginatively antedating their delight, and giving him that place in the calendar of their personal experience which belongs to him in the order of our poetic history.

And the feeling is a true one, for although intensity be the great characteristic of all genius, and the power of the poet is measured by his ability to renew the charm of freshness in what is outworn and habitual, yet there is something in Chaucer which gives him a personal property in the epithet "vernal," and makes him seem always to go hand in hand with May.

In our New England especially, where May-day is a mere superstition and the Maypole a poor half-hardy exotic which shivers in an east wind almost as sharp as Endicott's axe,— where frozen children, in unseasonable muslin, celebrate the floral games with nosegays from the milliner's, and winter reels back, like shattered Lear, bringing the dead spring in his arms, her budding breast and wan dilustered cheeks all overblown with the drifts and frosty streaks of his white beard,— where even Chanticleer, whose sap mounts earliest in that dawn of the year, stands dumb beneath the dripping eaves of his harem, with his melancholy tail at half-mast,— one has only to take down a volume of Chaucer, and forthwith he can scarce step without crushing a daisy, and the sunshine flickers on small new leaves that throb thick with song of merle and mavis. A breath of spring blows out of the opening lines of the "Canterbury Tales" that seems to lift the hair upon our brow:

> When that Aprile with his showers soote
> The drought of March hath pierced to the roote,
> And bathed every vein in that licour
> Of whose virtue engendered is the flour;

> When Zephirus eke with his sweet breath
> Enspired hath in every holt and heath
> The tender croppes; and the younge sun
> Hath in the Ram half of his course yrun;
> And little fowles maken melodie,
> That slepen all the night with open eye,
> So nature pricketh them in their courages.

Even Shakspeare, who comes after everybody has done his best and seems to say, "Here, let me take hold a minute and show you how to do it," could not mend that. With Chaucer, the sun seems never to have run that other half of his course in the Ram, but to have stood still there and made one long spring-day of his life.

Chaucer was probably born in 1328, seven years after the death of Dante, and he certainly died in 1400, having lived consequently seventy-two years. Of his family we know nothing. He was educated either at Oxford or Cambridge, or at neither of these famous universities. He was, perhaps, a student at the Inner Temple, on the books of which a certain phantasmagoric Mr. Buckley had read a record that "Geoffrey Chaucer was fined two shillings for beating a Franciscan friar in Fleet street."

In the thirty-ninth year of his age he received from Edward III a pension of twenty marks (equal to $1000 now), and afterwards a grant of a pitcher of wine daily, and the custody of a ward which gave £104 a year, and two places in the customs. In the last year of Edward III he was one of three envoys sent to France to negotiate a marriage between the Prince of Wales and a daughter of the French King. Richard II confirmed his pension of twenty marks, and granted him another of like amount instead of the daily wine.

Chaucer married Philippa Pycard or De la Roet, sister of Katherine Swynford, the third wife of John of Gaunt. By this connection he is supposed to have become a favorer of Wycliffe's doctrines, and was in some way concerned in the insurrection of John of Northampton, which seems to have had for its object some religious reform. He was forced to fly into Holland, and is said to have made his peace at last by betraying his companions. I think one's historical comfort is not disturbed by refusing to credit this story, especially as it stains the fame of a great poet, and, if character may ever be judged from writings, a good man. We may grant that he broke the Franciscan friar's head in Fleet street, if it were only for the alliteration, but let us doubt that he ever broke his faith. It is very doubtful whether he was such stuff as martyrs are made of. Plump men, though nature would seem to have marked them as more combustible, seldom go to the stake, but rather your lean fellows, who can feel a fine satisfaction in not burning well to spite the Philistines.

At this period of his life Chaucer is thought to have been in straitened circumstances, but a new pension and a yearly pipe of wine were granted him by Richard II, and on the accession of Henry IV these were confirmed, with a further pension of forty marks. These he only lived a year to enjoy, dying October 25, 1400.

The most poetical event in Chaucer's life the critics have, of course, endeavored to take away from us. This is his meeting with Petrarch, to which he alludes in the prologue to the Clerk's "Tale of Griseldis." There is no reason for doubting this that I am able to discover, except that it is so pleasing to think of, and that Chaucer affirms it. Chaucer's embassy to Italy was in 1373, the last year of Petrarch's life, and it was in this very year that Petrarch first read the "Decameron." In his letter to Boccaccio he says: "The touching story of Griseldis has been ever since laid up in my memory that I may relate it in my conversations with my friends." We are forced to believe so many things that ought never to have happened that the heart ought to be allowed to recompense itself by receiving as fact, without too close a scrutiny of the evidence, whatever deserved to take place so truly as this did. Reckoning back, then, by the finer astronomy of our poetic instinct, we find that a conjunction of these two stars of song did undoubtedly occur in that far-off heaven of the Past.

On the whole, we may consider the life of Chaucer as one of the happiest, and also the most fortunate, that ever fell to the lot of poets. In the course of it he must have been brought into relation with all ranks of men. He had been a student of books, of manners, and of countries. In his description of the Clerk of Oxford, in which there is good ground for thinking that he alludes to some of his own characteristics, he says:

> For him was liefer have at his bed's head
> A twenty books clothed in black or red,
> Of Aristotle and his philosophy,
> Than robes rich, or fiddle or psaltery.
> But albeit that he was a philosopher,
> Yet had he but a little gold in coffer;
> Of study took he the most care and heed,
> Not a word spake he more than there was need;
> And that was said in form and reverence,
> And short and quick, and full of high sentence;
> Sounding in moral virtue was his speech,
> And gladly would he learn, and gladly teach.

What a pleasant, companionable nature the last verse testifies to. The portrait of Chaucer, too, is perhaps more agreeable than that of any other English poet. The downcast, meditative eyes, the rich mouth, and the beautiful broad brow drooping with the weight of thought, and yet with an eternal youth and freshness shining out of it as from the morning forehead of a boy, are all remarkable, and their harmony with each other in a placid tenderness not less so.

Chaucer's beginnings as an author were translations from the French and Italian. Imitations they should rather be called, for he put *himself* into them, and the mixture made a new poem. He helped himself without scruple from every quarter. And, indeed, there is nothing more clear than that the great poets are not sudden prodigies, but slow results. Just as an oak profits by the foregone lives of immemorial vegetable races, so we may be sure that the genius of every remembered poet drew the forces that built it up from the decay of a whole forest of forgotten ones. And in proportion as the genius is vigorous and original will its indebtedness be; will it strike its roots deeper into the past and into remoter fields in search of the virtue that must sustain it.

Accordingly, Chaucer, like Shakspeare, invented

almost nothing. Wherever he found anything directed to Geoffrey Chaucer he took it and made the most of it. Indeed, the works of the great poets teach us to hold invention somewhat cheap. The Provençal rhymers did the best to invent things that nobody ever thought of before, and they succeeded in producing what nobody ever thought of again. He must be a very great poet indeed who can afford to say anything new.

In the great poets I think there is always a flavor of race or country which gives them a peculiar nearness to those of the same blood, and where the face of the individual nature is most marked, it will be found that the type of family is also most deeply stamped. It is remarkable that Chaucer, who probably spoke French as often and as familiarly as English, who levied his contributions upon Norman, Italian, and Latin writers, should yet have become (with an exception) the most truly English of our poets.

In endeavoring to point out what seem to be the peculiar characteristics of Chaucer, I think we shall find one of the chief to be this — that he is the first poet who has looked to nature as a motive of conscious emotion. Accordingly, his descriptions are always simple and addressed to the eye rather than to the mind, or to the fancy rather than to the imagination. Very often he is satisfied with giving a list of flowers with no epithet, or one expressive of color or perfume only.

Mr. Lowell here read a number of passages from the "Assembly of Fowls" and other poems of Chaucer, with an extract from Spenser.

Now I observe that all Chaucer's epithets are primary, or such as give birth to the feeling; and all Shakspeare's secondary, or such as the feeling gives birth to. In truth, Shakspeare's imagination is always dramatic, even in his narrative poems, and it was so abundant that the mere overflow of it has colored the very well-springs of the English language, and especially of English poetry. On Chaucer, nature seems to have always smiled (except in winter, which he cordially hated), and no rumor of man's fall appears to have reached the trees and birds and flowers. Nature has taken to thinking lately, and a moral jumps up out of a blossom, like a jack-in-a-box.

Another characteristic which we find in all the poems where Chaucer speaks in his own person is a sentiment of *seclusion*. He always dreams of walking in a park or a garden walled-in on every side. It is not narrowness but privacy that he delights in, and a certain feeling of generous limitation. In this his poems are the antithesis of

Milton's, which always give a feeling of great spaces.

In description it would be hard to find Chaucer's superior. His style is distinguished always by an energetic simplicity, which is a combination exceedingly rare. It was apparently natural to him. But when he is describing anything that he loves, there is an inexpressible tenderness, as if his eyes filled with tears. His narrative flows on like one of our inland rivers, sometimes hastening a little, and in its eddies seeming to run sunshine; sometimes lingering smoothly, while here and there a beautiful quiet thought, a pure feeling, a golden-hearted verse opens as quietly as a water-lily, and makes no ripple. In modern times the desire for startling expression is so strong that people hardly think a thought is good for anything unless it goes off with a *pop* like a gingerbeer cork.

In Chaucer's pathetic passages (and they are many), the presence of *pity* is a thing to be noticed — and the more so as he is the best pathetic story-teller among the English, and, except Dante, among the modern poets. Chaucer, when he comes to the sorrow of his story, seems to croon over the thoughts, and soothe them, and handle them with a pleasant compassionateness, as a child treats a wounded bird which he cannot make up his heart to let go, and yet fears to close his fingers too firmly upon.

Mr. Lowell, in illustration, read from the "Man of Law's Tale," and other of the poems.

What I have said of Chaucer's pathos is equally true of his humor. It never *invades* a story, but *pervades* it. It circulates through all his comic tales like lively blood, and never puddles on the surface any unhealthy spots of extravasation. And this I take to be the highest merit of narrative — diffusion without diffuseness.

I have not spoken yet of Chaucer's greatest work, the "Canterbury Tales." He has been greatly commended for his skill in the painting of character, and, indeed, nothing too good can be said of him in this respect. But I think it is too much the fashion to consider Chaucer as one of those Flemish painters who are called realists because they never painted the reality, but only the *material*. It is true that Chaucer is as minute in his costume as if he were illuminating a missal. Nothing escapes him — the cut of the beard, the color of the jerkin, the rustiness of the sword. He could not help this, his eye for the picturesque is so quick and sure. But in drawing the character it is quite otherwise. Here his style is large and free, and he emphasizes, but not too strongly, those points only which are essential, and which give variety to his picture without any loss to the keeping. For he did not forget that he was painting history and not a portrait. If his character of the good parson (which still stands not only unmatched but unapproached by the many later attempts at the same thing) seem an exception, it is yet in truth a confirmation of what I have said. For, in this case, for the very sake of *keeping*, it was necessary to be more full and careful, because the *good* parson alone must balance the friar, the pardoner, and all the other clerical personages who are almost unmixedly evil. Justice is always a leading quality in great minds, and by this single figure on one side and the group on the other Chaucer satirizes the Church, as it can only be satirized, by showing that it contrasts with that true religion with which it should be identical. And was there ever anything so happy as Chaucer's satire? Commonly satire is unhappy, but Chaucer's is positively more kindly than the panegyric of some poets.

In calling Chaucer *genial* I chose the word with forethought. This geniality made it impossible that his satire should be intellectual. The satire of the intellect deals with the outside only, trying the thing satirized by a rigid standard. But it results from Chaucer's genial temperament that justice in him is so equipoised by love that it becomes mercy, which is the point of rest between absolute law and human frailty. Therefore Chaucer, properly speaking, is not a satirist but a humorist; in other words, his satire is imaginative, and thus, in perfect subordination to narrative (though not to dramatic) art, he makes his characters satirize themselves. I suppose that no humorist ever makes anybody so thoroughly an object of satire as himself — but then one always satirizes himself kindly because he sees all sides. Falstaff is an example of this. Now this is just the character of imaginative or humorous satire, that the humorist enters his subject, assumes his consciousness, and works wholly from within. Accordingly when Chaucer makes his Frere or Pardoner expose all his own knaveries, we feel not as if he said, "See what a precious scamp this fellow is," but "This is the way *we* poor devils play fantastic tricks before high heaven." The butt of the humorist is Man (including himself and us); the butt of the satirist is always individual man. The humorist says *we*; the moralist and satirist, *thou*. Here is the strength of the great imaginative satirist of modern times, Mr. Thackeray.

In satire, the antithesis of Chaucer is Pope; as a painter of life and manners, Crabbe, who had great powers of observation without imagination. Therefore what is simplicity in Chaucer is poverty in Crabbe.

Chaucer is the first great poet who held up a mirror to contemporary life in its objectivity, and for the mere sake of its picturesqueness — that is, he is the first great poet who has treated To-day as if it were as good as Yesterday. Dante wrote life also, but it was his own life, and what is more, his own interior life. All his characters are represented in their relation to *that*. But Chaucer reflected life in its large sense — the life of *men*, from the knight to the ploughman. Thus it is that he always quietly and naturally rises above the Conventional into the Universal. And so his great poem lives forever in that perennial contemporaneousness which is the great privilege of genius. Thus the man of genius has a double immortality — in heaven and on earth at the same time; and this is what makes it good to *be* a genius at all, that their beauty and their goodness live after them, and every generation of men can say of them — They are *our* friends also.

I know not how to sum up what we feel about Chaucer except by saying, what would have pleased him most, that we *love* him. I would write on the first page of his volume the inscription which he puts over the gate in his "Assembly of Fowls":

> Through me men go into the blissful place
> Of the heart's heal, and deadly woundes cure;
> Through me men go into the welle of Grace,
> Where green and lusty May shall ever endure.
> This is the way to all good aventure;
> Be glad thou reader, and thy sorrow offcast.
> All open am I, pass in, and hye thee fast.

LECTURE VI

SPENSER

(*Friday Evening, January* 26, 1855)

VI

CHAUCER had been in his grave one hundred and fifty years before England had secreted choice material enough to produce another great poet. Or, perhaps, we take it for granted that Nature understands her own business too well to make such productions cheap. Beauty, we know, has no charm like that of its eternal unexpectedness, and the best delight is that which blossoms from a stem of bare and long days.

Or is it that the spirit of man, of every race of men, has its fatal ebbs and floods, its oscillations between the fluid ideal and the solid matter-of-fact, so that the doubtful line of shore between is in one generation a hard sandy actuality, with only such resemblances of beauty as a dead sea-moss here and there, and in the next is whelmed with those graceful curves of ever-gaining, ever-receding foam, and that dance of joyous spray which knows not, so bright is it, whether it be sea or sunshine.

What English Poetry was between Chaucer and Spenser there is no need to say. Scotland had given birth to two or three poets of that kind which is qualified by the epithet *national*, which is as much as saying that they took account only of the universe to the north-northeast corner of human nature instead of the whole circumference of it. England in the meanwhile had been enriched with Sternhold and Hopkins, but on the whole, the most important event between the death of Chaucer and the publication of the "Faëry Queene" was the introduction of blank verse. Perhaps the blank poetry suggested it.

Before the "Faëry Queene," also, two long poems were printed and popular — the "Mirror for Magistrates," and "Albion's England." How the first of these was ever read it is hard to conceive, unless we accept the theory of some theologians that our earth is only a kind of penal colony where men are punished for sins committed in some previous state of existence. The other was the work of one Warner, a conveyancer, and has a certain philological value now from its abounding in the popular phrases of the day. It is worth notice, also, as containing the most perfect example in the English language of what is called a conceit. It occurs in his account of Queen Elinor's treatment of Fair Rosamond:

> With that she dashed her on the lips
>   So dyed double red;
> Hard was the heart that struck the blow,
>   Soft were the lips that bled.

Which is nonsense and not poetry, though Dr. Percy admired it. Dr. Donne, and the poets whom Dr. Johnson called metaphysical (as if all poets are not so), is thought to be full of conceits. But the essence of a conceit is not in a comparison being far-fetched,—the imagination can make fire and water friendly when it likes,—but in playing upon the meanings of two words where one is taken in a metaphorical sense. This is a mark of the superficial mind always; whereas Donne's may be called a subterficial one, which went down to the roots of thought instead of playing with its blossoms.

Not long after the "Faëry Queene" were published the "Polyolbion" of Drayton, and the "Civil Wars" of Daniel. Both of these men were respectable poets (especially Drayton), but neither of them could reconcile poetry with gazetteering or chronicle-making. They are as unlike as a declaration in love and a declaration in law.

This was the period of the Saurians in English Poetry, interminable poems, book after book and canto after canto, like far-stretching *vertebræ*, prodigious creatures that rendered the earth unfit for the dwelling of Man. They are all dead now, the unwieldy monsters — ichthyo-, plesio-, and megalosauri — they all sleep well, and their huge remains are found imbedded in those vast morasses, the "Collections of the Poets." We wonder at the length of face and general atra-bilious look that mark the portraits of that generation; but it is no marvel when even the poetry was such downright hard work. Poems of this sort might have served to while away the three-centuried evening of antediluvian lives. It is easy to understand how our ancestors could achieve great things when they encountered such hardships for mere amusement. If we agree with Horace in pitying the pre-Homeric heroes because they were without poets, we may sincerely commiserate our forefathers of that generation because they had them. The reading of one of these productions must have been nearly as long a business as the taking of Troy, and deserved a poet to sing it. Perhaps fathers, when their time on earth was up, folded the leaf down and left the task to be finished by their sons — a dreary inheritance.

The popularity of such works shows the insatiable thirst of the human soul for something which at least tried to be beyond mere matter-of-fact. This thirst for the ideal transmuted these books into poetry, just as the eternal drought of the desert turns muddy water into nectar, and the famine of the shipwrecked sailor gives a flavor beyond French cookery to a soup made of old shoes (*potage aux choux*). But meanwhile Nature, who loves surprises, was quietly preparing a noble one. A new poet had been born, and came upon that arid century fresh and dewy as out of the first dawn that waked the birds in Eden. A great poet is always impossible — till he comes, and then he seems the simplest thing in the world to the commentators. He got this notice here and the other there; similar subjects had been treated by such a one, and the metre first used by another. They give us all the terms of the equation; satisfy us that a plus b minus c equals x, only we are left in the dark as to what x is. The genius continues to be an unknown quantity. The great poet is as original as to-morrow's sunrise, which will take the old clouds and vapors, and little household smokes of our poor, worn-out earth to make a miracle out of, and transfigure the old hills and fields and houses with the enchantment of familiar novelty. It is this power of being at once familiar and novel that distinguishes the primary poets. They give us a new heaven and a new earth without the former things having passed away,—whose very charm is that they have not,—a new heaven and a new earth that we can possess by the fireside, in the street, and the counting-room.

Edmund Spenser was born, like Chaucer, in London, in 1553, when Cervantes was six years old. That sixteenth century was a miraculous one. Scarce any other can show such a concurrence of great brains. Mothers must have expected an attack of genius among their children, as we look for measles or whooping-cough now. While Spenser was yet delving over the *propria quæ maribus*, Shakspeare was stretching out his baby arms and trying to get the moon to play with, and the little Bacon, chewing upon his coral, had already learned the impenetrability of matter. It almost takes one's breath away to think that at the same time "Hamlet" and the "Novum Organon" were at the mercy of teething and the scarlet fever, unless, indeed, destiny takes care to lock the doors against those child-stealing gypsies when she leaves such precious things about.

Of Spenser's personal history we know very little. He was educated at Cambridge, where he took the degree of Master of Arts in 1576. He is supposed to have passed the three following years with some relations in the country, where he wrote verses and fell in love with a lady whom he calls Rosalind, and of whom we know nothing further unless we are satisfied to take the portrait which Shakspeare has associated forever with the name which he complimented by adopting. He is said to have been employed to carry a despatch or two, but Lord Burleigh did not fancy him. Poor Lord Burleigh! Sidney and Raleigh, however, were luckier. He was recommended to the great queen, and received at last a grant of Kilcolman Castle and three thousand acres of land in the south of Ireland. Here the "Faëry Queene" was in great part written. At last came a rebellion. The wild kernes and gallow-glasses had not the delicacy of the Emathian conqueror, and they burned the castle, from which Spenser and his wife with two of their children barely escaped, leaving an infant to perish in the flames. Spenser came to London and died brokenhearted three months afterward, on the 16th of January, 1599. That rare nature was like a Venice glass, meant only to mantle with the wine of the sunniest poetry. The first drop of poisonous sorrow shattered it.

In 1579 Spenser published the "Shepherd's Calendar," a series of twelve eclogues, one for each month in the year. In these poems he professedly imitated Chaucer, whom he called his master, but without much success. Even with the light reflected upon them from the lustre of his great poem, one can find but little in them that is not dull. There are indications in these poems, however, here and there, of a nice ear for harmony in verse.

Spenser was the pure sense of the Beautiful put into a human body only that it might have the means of communicating with men. His own description of Clarion, the butterfly in his "Muiopotmos," gives, perhaps, the best possible idea of his own character.

> Over the fields, in his frank lustiness,
>   And all the champaign o'er, he soared light
> And all the country wide he did possess,
> Feeding upon their pleasures bounteously,
> That none gainsay, and none did him envy.
>
> The woods, the rivers, and the meadows green,
>   With his air-cutting wings he measured wide,
> Nor did he leave the mountains bare unseen,
>   Nor the rank grassy fens' delights untried;
> But none of these, however sweet they been,
>   Mote please his fancy, or him cause to abide;
> His choiceful sense with every change doth flit,
> No common things may please a wavering wit.
>
> To the gay gardens his unstaid desire
>   Him wholly carried, to refresh his sprights;
> There lavish Nature, in her last attire,
>   Pours forth sweet odors and alluring sights;

SPENSER

And Art, with her contending, doth aspire
   To excel the natural with made delights,
And all that fair or pleasant may be found,
In riotous excess doth there abound.

There he arriving, round about doth flie,
   From bed to bed, from one to the other border,
And takes survey with curious busy eye,
   Of every flower and herb there set in order;
Now this, now that, he tasteth tenderly,
   Yet none of them he rudely doth disorder;
He with his feet their silken leaves displace,
But pastures on the pleasures of each place.

And evermore with most variety
   And change of sweetness (for all change is sweet),
He casts his glutton sense to satisfy,
   Now sucking of the sap of herbs most meet,
Or of the dew which yet on them doth lie,
   Now in the same bathing his tender feet;
And then he percheth on some branch thereby
To weather him, and his moist wings to dry.

And whatsoe'er of virtue good or ill,
   Grew in his garden fetched from far away,
Of every one he takes and tastes at will,
   And on their pleasures greedily doth prey;
Then, when he hath both played and fed his fill,
   In the warm sun he doth himself embay,
And there him rests in riotous suffisance
Of all his gladfulness and kingly joyance.

> What more felicity can fall a creature
>   Than to enjoy delight with liberty?
> And to be lord of all the works of Nature,
>   To reign in the air from earth to highest sky?
> To feed on flowers and weeds of glorious feature,
>   To take whatever thing doth please the eye?
> Who rests not pleased with such happiness
> Well worthy he to taste of wretchedness.

What poet has ever left us such a portrait of himself as this? In that butterfly Spenser has symbolized the purely poetical nature. It will be seen that there is no recognition of the moral sense whatever. The poetic nature considered abstractly craves only beauty and delight — without any thought beyond —

> And whatsoe'er *of virtue good or ill,*
> To feed on flowers and *weeds of glorious feature.*

The poetical temperament has nowhere been at once so exquisitely defined and illustrated. Among poets, Spenser stands for the temperament personified.

But how did it happen that this lightsome creature, whose only business was

> To reign in the air from earth to highest sky,

should have attempted in his greatest work to mix together two such incoherent things as sermon and poem? In the first place, the age out of which a man is born is the mother of his mind, and imprints her own likeness more or less clearly on the features of her child. There are two destinies from which no one can escape, his own idiosyncrasy, and that of the time in which he lives. Or shall we say that where the brain is in flower of its conceptions, the very air is full of thought-pollen, or some wandering bee will bring it, we know not from what far field, to hybridize the fruit?

In Spenser's time England was just going through the vinous stage of that Puritanic fermentation which became acetous in Milton, and putrefactive in the Fifth Monarchy men. Here was one motive. But, besides this, it is evident that Spenser's fancy had been colored by the Romances which were popular in his day; and these had all been allegorized by the monks, who turned them into prose. The adventure of the San Grail in the "Morte d'Arthur" reads almost like an extract from the "Pilgrim's Progress." Allegories were the fashion, and Spenser put one on as he did a ruff, not because it was the most convenient or becoming thing in the world, but because other people did.

Another reason is probably to be found in the

nature of the man himself. The poetical temperament, when it comes down to earth and mingles with men, is conscious of a certain weakness. On the unsubstantial skyey floors of its own ideal world it walks firmly enough, and speaks the native language of the shadowy population there. But there is a knell at which that beautiful land dissolves like the baseless fabric of a vision — and that is the dinner bell. The poetical temperament becomes keenly conscious that it also has a stomach. It must dine, and commonly it likes rather better dinners than other people. To this end it must carry its wares to market where the understanding is master. Will the understanding pay hard money for the flowers of speech? Only what is practical will do there. "Fine words," grumbles the Understanding proverbially, "butter no parsnips; and then, to make the matter worse, the *parsnips* are *ideal*." "But, my dear sir," remonstrates Temperament mildly — "Dear me no dears," growls Understanding. "Everybody must earn his own salt — I do." "Let me read you my beautiful poem." "Can't comprehend a word of it. The only language I know a word of is my old mother tongue, the *useful*. Look at the towns and ships I've built. Nothing ideal *there*, you'll find. Ideal, I suppose, is a new-fangled way of spelling idle. It won't go here." Suddenly the *useful* seems a very solid and powerful thing to our poor friend, the Poetic Temperament. It begins to feel a little absurd in talking enthusiasm to such a matter-of-fact generation. The problem is how to translate the ideal into the useful. How shall Master Edmund Spenser make himself comprehensible to Master John Bull? He will try a picture-book, and a moral one, too — he will write an Allegory.

Allegory is the Imagination of the Understanding, or what it supposes to be, which is the same thing. It is the ideal in words of one syllable, illustrated with cuts, and adapted to the meanest comprehension.

Spenser was a good and pure-minded man, and wished probably to combine the sacred office of Teacher with that of Poet. The preaching part of him came afterwards in Jeremy Taylor, who was Spenser with his singing-robes off.

Spenser's mind was so thoroughly imbued with the beautiful that he makes even the Cave of Mammon a place one would like to live in.

I think it is the want of *human* interest that makes the "Faëry Queene" so little read. Hazlitt has said that nobody need be afraid of the allegory; it will not bite them, nor meddle with them unless they meddle with it. It was the first poem

I ever read, and I had no suspicion of any double meaning in it. If we think of the moral as we read it will injure the effect of the poem, because we have an instinctive feeling that Beauty includes its own moral, and does not need to have it stuck on.

Charles Lamb made the most comprehensive criticism upon Spenser when he called him the "poets' poet." This was a magic mirror which he held up to life, where only shapes of loveliness are reflected. A joyous feeling of the beautiful thrills through the whole poem.

I think that Spenser has come nearer to expressing the unattainable something than any other poet. He is so purely a poet of beauty that with him the meaning does not modulate the music of the verse, but the music is a great part of the meaning. No poet is so splendidly superfluous as he. He knows too well that in poetry *enough* is parsimony. The delight of beauty is that it is like a fountain, forever changing, forever the same, and forever more than full.

Spenser has characterized his own poem in the song which the Sirens sing to Sir Guyon in the twelfth canto of the second book. The whole passage also may be called his musical as distinguished from his picturesque style.

In reading Spenser one may see all the great galleries of painting without stepping over his threshold. Michael Angelo is the only artist that he will not find there. It may be said of him that he is not a narrative poet at all, that he tells no stories, but paints them.

I have said that among our poets Spenser stands for the personification of the poetic sense and temperament. In him the senses were so sublimed and etherealized, and sympathized so harmoniously with an intellect of the subtlest quality that, with Dr. Donne, we "could almost say his body thought." This benign introfusion of sense and spirit it is which gives his poetry the charm of crystalline purity without loss of warmth. He is ideal without being merely imaginative; he is sensuous without any suggestion of flesh and blood. He is full of feeling, and yet of such a kind that we can neither call it mere intellectual perception of what is fair and good and touching, nor associate it with that throbbing warmth which leads us to call sensibility by its human name of heart. In the world into which he carries us there is neither space nor time, and so far it is purely intellectual, but then it is full of form and color and all earthly gorgeousness, and so far it is sensual. There are no men and women in it, and yet it throngs with airy and immortal shapes that have the likeness of men and women.

To appreciate fully the sensuous intellectuality of this divine poet, compare him for a moment with Pope, who had an equal subtlety of brain without the joyous poetic sense. Pope's mind was like a perfectly clear mirror hung in a drawing-room, and reflecting with perfect precision of outline and vividness of coloring, not man, but good society, every grace and every folly that belong not to human nature in its broad meaning, but as it is subordinated by fashion. But Spenser is like a great calm pool that lies brooding in delicious reverie over its golden sands in some enchanted world. If we look into it we know not if we see the shadows of clouds and trees and castles, of bright-armored knights and peerless dames that linger and are gone; or whether those pellucid depths are only a mysterious reservoir, where all the fairest dreams of our youth, dreams that were like hopes, and hopes that were but dreams, are visionarily gathered. Anon a ripple, born of no breeze, but of the poet's own conscious joy, startles it into a dance of sunshine that fades away around its shores in a lapsing murmur that seems the shadow of music rather than its substance.

So entirely are beauty and delight the element of Spenser, that whenever in the "Faëry Queene" you come upon a thought or moral reflection it gives you a shock of unpleasant surprise, a kind of grit, as when one's teeth close upon a bit of gravel in a dish of strawberries and cream. He is the most fluent of our poets. Sensation passing over through emotion into reverie is the characteristic of his manner.

And to read him puts one in the condition of reverie — a state of mind in which one's thoughts and feelings float motionless as you may see fishes do in a swift brook, only vibrating their fins enough to keep themselves from being swept down the current, while their bodies yield to all its curvings and quiver with the thrills of its fluid and sinuous delight. It is a luxury beyond luxury itself, for it is not only dreaming awake, but dreaming without the trouble of doing it yourself; letting it be done for you, in truth, by the finest dreamer that ever lived, who has the art of giving you all his own visions through the medium of music.

Of the versification of Spenser we need attempt no higher praise than that it belonged to him. If we would feel the infinite variety of the Spenserian stanza, as Spenser uses it, its musical intricacies, its long, sliding cadences, smooth as the green slope on the edge of Niagara, we have only to read verses of the same measure by other poets.

As showing his pathos, Mr. Lowell read Una's lament on her desertion by the Red Cross Knight, and other pieces, calling attention particularly to the fact that his females were not women, like those of Shakspeare, but ideal beings.

We are accustomed to apologize for the grossness of our favorite old authors by saying that their age was to blame, and not they. Spenser needs no such excuses. He is the most perfect gentleman among poets. Through that unrefined time, when ladies drank a quart of ale for breakfast, and even Hamlet can say a coarse thing to Ophelia, Spenser passes pure and chaste as another Sir Galahad.

Whoever can endure unmixed delight, whoever can tolerate music, and painting, and poetry, all in one, whoever wishes to be rid of thought and to let the busy anvils of the brain be silent for a time, let him read in the "Faëry Queene." There is a land of pure Heart's Ease where no ache or sorrow of spirit can enter. If there be any poet whom we can love and feel grateful toward, it is Edmund Spenser.

LECTURE VII

MILTON

(Tuesday Evening, January 30, 1855)

VII

BETWEEN Spenser and Milton occurred the most truly imaginative period of English poetry. It is the time of Shakspeare and of the other dramatists only less than he. It seems to have been the moment in which the English mind culminated.

Even if we subtract Shakspeare, the age remains without a parallel. The English nature was just then giving a great heave and yearn toward freedom in politics and religion, and literature could not fail to partake of the movement.

A wave of enthusiasm seemed to break over England; all that was poetical in the people found expression in deed or word. Everything tasted of it — sermons and speeches as well as verses. The travelers could not write a dry journal, but they somehow blundered into a poetical phrase that clings to the memory like a perfume. The sensations of men were as fresh as Adam's, and the words they found to speak them in could be beautiful or fragrant with as little effort as it costs violets to be blue.

It is a remarkable fact that the poetry of Shakspeare is at the same time more English and more universally human than any that was ever written. The two great poets who came before Shakspeare had both of them enlarged the revenues of the English muse. Chaucer had added character and incident, and had shown the capacities of the language and of the metre. Spenser left it enriched with a luxury of diction, with harmony of verse, and with the lovely images of the classical mythology. But Shakspeare came in like an unthrift heir. He squandered everything. From king to clown he used up all character; there is no passion, or fancy, or feeling that he has not spent; no question of philosophy, morals, politics, or metaphysics that he has not solved; he poured out all the golden accumulations of diction like water. And his younger brethren, the other dramatists, helped him. What was there left? Certainly, this wonderful being has expressed every sentiment, every thought, that is universal in its relations. All the poetry of this world he exhausted. Accordingly, in the time immediately following this splendidly imaginative period, we find only a development of fancy under one or other of its disguises. Fancy deals with limited and personal experiences, and interests us by the grace or perfectness of its expression of these. The Dramatists were tremendously in earnest, as they had need to be, to please a people who were getting in earnest themselves. But now the time itself was preparing a drama, and on no mimic scene, but with England for a stage and with all Europe for spectators. A real historical play was in rehearsal, no petty war of York and Lancaster, but the death-grapple of two eras. The time was in travail with the Ishmael of Puritanism who, exiled from his father's house, was to found here in this Western wilderness an empire for himself and his wandering descendants. England herself was turning poet, and would add her rhapsody to the great epic of the nations.

That was a day of earnest and painful thinking, and poetical temperaments naturally found relief in turning away from actual life to the play of the fancy. We find no trace of high imagination here. Certainly, Herbert and Vaughan and even Quarles are sometimes snatched into something above common fancy by religious fervor, but how cold and experimental is the greater part of their poetry — not poetry, indeed, but devotional exercises in verse. Cowley wrote imaginary love-songs to an imaginary mistress, and Waller the same sort of stuff to a real one. Catullus revived in Herrick, a country parson. Wither, a Puritan, wrote some poems full of nature and feeling, and remarkable for purity of sentiment. Donne, a deep thinker, carried on his anatomical studies into his verse, and dissected his thoughts and feelings to the smallest nerve. A great many nice things got said, no doubt, and many charming little poems were written — but the *great* style appears no longer.

It was during this lull, as we may call it, that followed the mighty day of the Dramatists, that Milton was growing up. He was born in London on the ninth of December, 1608, and was therefore in his eighth year when Shakspeare died. His father was of a good family, which still adhered to the Roman Catholic faith. What is of more importance, he was disinherited by *his* father for having adopted Puritan principles; and he was a excellent musician. Milton was very early an indefatigable student, even in his twelfth year seldom leaving his books before midnight. At the university he was distinguished as a Latin scholar and writer of Latin verses. He was intended for the Church, but had already formed opinions of his own which put conformity out of the question. He was by nature an Independent, and could not, as he says, "subscribe *slave.*"

Leaving the university in 1632, he passed the five following years in a studious seclusion at his father's house at Horton, in Buckinghamshire. During these five years he wrote most of his smaller poems. In 1638 he set out for Italy. The most important events of his stay in that country were his meetings with Galileo, and the Marquis Manso, who had been Tasso's friend. After refreshing his Protestantism at Geneva, he passed through France and came back to England to find the Civil War already begun.

Dr. Johnson sneers at Milton for having come home from Italy because he could not stay abroad while his countrymen were struggling for their freedom, and then quietly settling down as a teacher of a few boys for bread. It might, with equal reason, have been asked of the Doctor why, instead of writing "Taxation no Tyranny," he did not volunteer in the war against the rebel American provinces? Milton sacrificed to the cause he thought holy something dearer to him than life—the hope of an earthly immortality in a great poem. He suffered his eyes to be put out for the sake of his country as deliberately as Scaevola thrust his hand into the flame. He gave to freedom something better than a sword—words that were victories. Around the memories of Bradshaw and his illustrious brethren his deathless soldiery still pitch their invincible tents, still keep their long-resounding march, sure warders against obloquy and oblivion.

After the death of Cromwell, Milton continued faithful to republicanism, and on the very eve of the Restoration published his last political tract, showing a short and easy way to establish a Christian commonwealth. He had long ago quarreled with the Presbyterians in discipline, and separated from the Independents in doctrine. For many years he did not go within any church and had become a Unitarian. He had begun "Paradise Lost" in 1658, and after the Restoration, with a broken fortune, but with a constancy which nothing could break, shattered in health, blind, and for a time in danger, he continued the composition of it. It was complete in 1665, when Elwood, the Quaker, had the reading of it, and it was published in 1667.

The translation of the Bible had to a very great extent Judaized the Puritan mind. England was no longer England, but Israel. Those fierce enthusiasts could always find Amalek and Philistia in the men who met them in the field, and one horn or the other of the beast in every doctrine of their theological adversaries. The spiritual provincialism of the Jewish race found something congenial in the Anglo-Saxon intellect. This element of the Puritan character appears in Milton also, as in that stern sonnet:

> Avenge, O Lord, thy slaughtered saints, whose bones
>   Lie scattered on the Alpine mountains cold,
>   Even them who kept thy truth so pure of old
> When all our fathers worshipped stocks and stones.

In Milton's prose there is a constant assertion of himself as a man set apart to a divine ministry. He seems to translate himself out of Hebrew into English. And yet so steeped was he in Greek culture that it is sometimes hard to say whether he would rather call himself the messenger of Jehovah or the son of Phœbus. Continually the fugitive mists of dialectics are rent, and through them shine down serene and solemn peaks that make us feel that we are encamped about by the sacred mounts of song, but whether of Palestine or of Greece is doubtful. We may apply to Milton what Schiller says of the poet, " Let the kind divinity snatch the suckling from his mother's breast, nourish him with the milk of a better age, and let him come to maturity beneath a distant Grecian sky. Then when he has become a man let him return, a foreign shape, into his century, not to delight it with his apparition, but terrible, like Agamemnon's son, to purify it."

I said that Milton had a sublime egotism. The egotism of a great character is inspiration because it generalizes self into universal law. It is a very different thing from the vulgar egotism of a little nature which contracts universal Law into self. The one expands with a feeling that it is a part of the law-making power, the other offers an amendment in town-meeting as if it came from Sinai. Milton's superb conception of himself enters into all he does; if *he* is blind, it is with excess of light—it is a divine favor, an overshadowing with angel's wings. Phineus and Tiresias are admitted among the prophets because they, too, had lost their sight. There is more merit in the blindness of Mæonides than in his "Iliad" or "Odyssey." If the structure of *his* mind is undramatic, why, then the English drama is barbarous, and he will write a tragedy on a Greek model with blind Samson for a hero.

It results from this that no great poet is so uniformly self-conscious as he. Dante is individual rather than self-conscious, and the cast-iron Dante becomes pliable as a field of grain at the breath of Beatrice, and his whole nature, rooted as it is, seems to flow away in waves of sunshine. But Milton never lets himself go for a moment. As other poets are possessed by their theme, so is he always self-possessed, his great theme being Milton, and his duty being that of interpreter between John Milton and the world. I speak it reverently—he was worth translating.

We should say of Shakspeare that he had the power of transforming himself into everything, and of Milton that he had that of transforming everything into himself. He is the most learned of poets. Dante, it is true, represents all the scholarship of his age, but Milton belonged to a more learned age, was himself one of the most learned men in it, and included Dante himself among his learning. No poet is so indebted to books and so little to personal observation as he. I thought once that he had created out of his own consciousness those exquisite lines in "Comus":

> A thousand fantasies
> Begin to throng into my memory
> Of calling shapes, and beckoning shadows dire,
> And airy tongues that syllable men's names
> On sands and shores and desert wildernesses.

But I afterwards found that he had built them up out of a dry sentence in Marco Polo's "Travels." The wealth of Milton in this respect is wonderful. He subsidizes whole provinces of learning to spend their revenues upon one lavish sentence, and melts history, poetry, mythology, and philosophy together to make the rich Miltonic metal of a single verse.

The first noticeable poem of Milton is his "Hymn of the Nativity," and the long-enwoven harmony of the versification is what chiefly deserves attention in it. It is this which marks the advent of a new power into English poetry.

In Spenser meaning and music are fused together; in Shakspeare the meaning dominates always (and I intend the sentiment as included in the word meaning); but in Milton the music is always a primary consideration. He is always as much musician as poet. And he is a harmonist, not a melodist. He loves great pomps and sequences of verse, and his first passages move like long processions, winding with sacred chant, and priestly robes rich with emblematic gold, and waving of holy banners, along the echoing aisles of some cathedral. Accordingly, no reader of Milton can fail to notice that he is fond of lists of proper names which can have only an acquired imaginative value, and in that way serve to excite our poetic sensibility, but which also are of deep musical significance.

This was illustrated by reading various passages from "Paradise Lost."

Another striking peculiarity of Milton is the feeling of *spaciousness* which his poetry gives us, and that not only in whole paragraphs, but even in single words. His mind was one which demanded illimitable room to turn in. His finest passages are those in which the imagination diffuses itself over a whole scene or landscape, or where it seems to circle like an eagle controlling with its eye broad sweeps of champaign and of sea, bathing itself in the blue streams of air, and seldom drawn earthward in the concentrated energy of its swoop.

This shows itself unmistakably in the epithets of his earlier poems. In "Il Penseroso," for example, where he hears

> The far-off curfew sound
> Over some *wide-watered* shore
> Swinging slow with sullen roar;

where he sees

> Gorgeous Tragedy
> In sceptered pall come sweeping by,

or calls up the great bards who have sung

> Of forests and enchantments drear
> Where more is meant than meets the ear.

Milton seems to produce his effects by exciting or dilating our own imaginations; and this excitement accomplished, he is satisfied. Shakspeare, on the other hand, seldom leaves any work to be done by the imagination of his readers; and after we have enjoyed the total effect of a passage, we may always study the particulars with advantage. Shakspeare never attaches any particular value to his thoughts, or images, or phrases, but scatters them with a royal carelessness. Milton seems always to respect his; he lays out broad avenues for the triumphal processions of his verse; covers the ground with tapestry inwoven with figures of mythology and romance; builds up arches rich with historic carvings for them to march under, and accompanies them with swells and cadences of inspiring music. "Paradise Lost" is full of what may be called *vistas* of verse. Notice, for example, how far off he begins when he is about to speak of himself — as at the beginning of the third book and of the seventh. When you read "Paradise Lost" the feeling you have is one of *vastness*. You float under a great sky brimmed with sunshine, or hung with constellations; the abyss of space is around you; thunders mutter on the horizon; you hear the mysterious sigh of an unseen ocean; and if the scene changes, it is with an elemental movement like the shifting of mighty winds. Of all books it seems most purely the work of a disembodied mind. Of all poets he could most easily afford to be blind; of all, his poetry owes least to the senses, except that of hearing; everything, except his music, came to him through a mental medium, and perhaps even that may have been intellectual—as in Beethoven, who composed behind the veil of deafness.

Milton is a remarkable instance of a great imaginative faculty fed by books instead of Nature. One has only to read the notes of the commentators upon his poems to see how perfectly he made whatever he took his own. Everything that he touches swells and towers into vastness. It is wonderful to see how, from the most withered and juiceless hint that he met in his reading, his grand images "rise like an exhalation"; how from the most hopeless-looking leaden box that he found in that huge drag-net with which he gathered everything from the waters of learning, he could conjure a tall genius to do his bidding.

That proud consciousness of his own strength, and confidence at the same time that he is the messenger of the Most High, never forsake him. It is they which give him his grand manner, and make him speak as if with the voice of a continent. He reverenced always the sacredness of his own calling and character. As poet, full of the lore of antiquity, and, as prophet, charged to vindicate the ways of God, it seems to me that I see the majestic old man laying one hand upon the shoulder of the Past, and the other upon that of the Future, and so standing sublimely erect above that abject age to pour his voice along the centuries. We are reminded of what is told of Firdusi, whose father on the night he was born dreamed he saw him standing in the middle of the earth and singing so loud and clear that he was heard in all four quarters of the heavens at once.

I feel how utterly inadequate any single lecture must be on such a theme, and how impossible it is to say anything about Milton in an hour. I have merely touched upon three or four points that seemed to me most characteristic of his style, for our concern with him is solely as a poet. Yet it would be an unpardonable reticence if I did not say, before I close, how profoundly we ought to reverence the grandeur of the man, his incorruptible love of freedom, his scholarly and unvulgar republicanism, his scorn of contemporary success, his faith in the future and in God, his noble frugality of life.

The noise of those old warfares is hushed; the song of Cavalier and the fierce psalm of the Puritan are silent now; the hands of his episcopal adversaries no longer hold pen or crozier—they and their works are dust; but he who loved truth more than life, who was faithful to the other world while he did his work in this; his seat is in that great cathedral whose far-echoing aisles are the ages whispering with blessed feet of the Saints, Martyrs, and Confessors of every clime and creed; whose bells sound only centurial hours; about whose spire crowned with the constellation of the cross no meaner birds than missioned angels hover; whose organ music is the various stops of endless changes breathed through by endless good; whose choristers are the elect spirits of all time, that sing, serene and shining as morning stars, the ever-renewed mystery of Creative Power.

LECTURE VIII

BUTLER

(Friday Evening, February 2, 1855)

VIII

NEITHER the Understanding nor the Imagination is sane by itself; the one becomes blank worldliness, the other hypochondria. A very little imagination is able to intoxicate a weak understanding, and this appears to be the condition of religious enthusiasm in vulgar minds. Puritanism, as long as it had a material object to look forward to, was strong and healthy. But Fanaticism is always defeated by success; the moment it is established in the repose of power, it necessarily crystallizes into cant and formalism around any slenderest threads of dogma; and if the intellectual fermentation continue after the spiritual has ceased, as it constantly does, it is the fermentation of putrefaction, breeding nothing but the vermin of incoherent and destructively-active metaphysic subtleties — the maggots, as Butler, condensing Lord Bacon, calls them, of corrupted texts. That wise man Oliver Cromwell has been reproached for desertion of principles because he recognized the truth that though enthusiasm may overturn a government, it can never carry on one. Our Puritan ancestors came to the same conclusion, and have been as unwisely blamed for it. While we wonder at the prophetic imagination of those heroic souls who could see in the little *Mayflower* the seeds of an empire, while we honor (as it can only truly be honored — by imitating) that fervor of purpose which could give up everything for principle, let us be thankful that they had also that manly English sense which refused to sacrifice *their* principles to the fantasy of every wandering Adoniram or Shear-Jashub who mistook himself for Providence as naturally and as obstinately as some lunatics suppose themselves to be tea-pots.

The imaginative side of Puritanism found its poetical expression in Milton and its prose in Bunyan. The intellectual vagaries of its decline were to have their satirist in Butler. He was born at Strensham in Worcestershire in 1612, the son of a small farmer who was obliged to pinch himself to afford his son a grammar-school education. It is more than doubtful whether he were ever at any university at all. His first employment was as clerk to Mr. Jeffereys, a Worcestershire justice of the peace, called by the poet's biographers an eminent one. While in this situation he employed his leisure in study, and in cultivating music and painting, for both of which arts he had a predilection. He next went into the family of the Countess of Kent, where he had the use of a fine library, and where he acted as amanuensis to John Selden — the mere drippings of whose learning were enough to make a great scholar of him. After this he was employed (in what capacity is unknown) in the house of Sir Samuel Luke, an officer of Cromwell, and a rigid Presbyterian. It was here that he made his studies for the characters of *Sir Hudibras* and his squire, *Ralpho*, and is supposed to have begun the composition of his great work. There is hardly anything more comic in "Hudibras" itself than the solemn Country Knight unconsciously furnishing clothes from his wardrobe, and a rope of his own twisting, to hang himself in eternal effigy with. Butler has been charged with ingratitude for having caricatured his employer; but there is no hint of any obligation he was under, and the service of a man like him must have been a fair equivalent for any wages.

On the other hand, it has been asserted that Butler did not mean Sir Samuel Luke at all, but a certain Sir Henry Rosewell, or a certain Colonel Rolle, both Devonshire men. And in confirmation of it we are told that Sir Hugh de Bras was the tutelary saint of Devonshire. Butler, however, did not have so far to go for a name, but borrowed it from Spenser.

He himself is the authority for the "conjecture," as it is called, that his hero and Sir Samuel Luke were identical. At the end of the first canto of part first of "Hudibras" occurs a couplet of which the last part of the second verse is left blank. This couplet, for want of attention to the accent, has been taken to be in ten-syllable measure, and therefore an exception to the rest of the poem. But it is only where we read it as a verse of four feet that the inevitable rhyme becomes perfectly Hudibrastic. The knight himself is the speaker:

> 'Tis sung there is a valiant Mameluke
> In foreign lands yclept (Sir Sam Luke)
> To whom we have been oft compared
> For person, parts, address and beard.

Butler died poor, but not in want, on the 25th of September, 1680, in his sixty-eighth year.

Butler's poem is commonly considered the type of the burlesque — that is, as the representative of the gravely ludicrous, which seems to occupy a kind of neutral ground between the witty and the humorous. But this is true of the form rather than the matter of the poem. Burlesque appears to be wit infused with animal spirits — satire for the mere fun of the thing, without any suggestion of intellectual disapproval, or moral indignation. True wit is a kind of instantaneous logic which gives us the *quod erat demonstrandum* without the intermediate steps of the syllogism. Coleridge, with admirable acuteness, has said that "there is such a thing as scientific wit." Therefore pure wit sometimes gives an intellectual pleasure without making us laugh. The wit that makes us laugh most freely is that which instantly accepts another man's premises, and draws a conclusion from them in its own favor. A country gentleman was once showing his improvements to the Prince de Ligne, and, among other things, pointed out to him a muddy spot which he called his lake. "It is rather shallow, is it not?" said the Prince. "I assure you, Prince, a man drowned himself in it." "Ah, he must have been a flatterer, then," answered De Ligne. Of the same kind is the story told of one of our old Massachusetts clergymen, Dr. Morse. At an association dinner a debate arose as to the benefit of whipping in bringing up children. The doctor took the affirmative, and his chief opponent was a young minister whose reputation for veracity was not very high. He affirmed that parents often did harm to their children by unjust punishment from not knowing the facts in the case. "Why," said he, "the only time my father ever whipped me was for telling the truth." "Well," retorted the doctor, "it cured you of it, did n't it?" In wit of this sort, there is always a latent syllogism.

Then there is the wit which detects an unintentional bit of satire in a word of double meaning; as where Sir Henry Wotton takes advantage of the phrase commonly used in his day to imply merely residence, and finds an under meaning in it, saying that "ambassadors were persons sent to *lie* abroad for the service of their prince."

On the other hand I think unconsciousness and want of intention, or at least the pretense of it, is more or less essential to the ludicrous. For this reason what may be called the wit of events is always ludicrous. Nothing can be more so, for example, than the Pope's sending a Cardinal's hat to John Fisher, Bishop of Rochester, which arrived in England after Henry VIII had taken off that prelate's head. So, when Dr. Johnson said very gravely one day, that he had *often thought* that if he had a harem he would dress all the ladies in white linen, the unintentional incongruity of the speech with the character of the great moralist threw Boswell into an ecstasy of laughter. Like this is the ludicrousness of Pope Paul III writing to the Council of Trent "that they should begin with original sin, observing yet a due respect unto the Emperor."

Captain Basil Hall, when he traveled in this country, found the Yankees a people entirely destitute of wit and humor. Perhaps our gravity, which ought to have put him on the right scent, deceived him. I do not know a more perfect example of wit than something which, as I have heard, was said to the captain himself. Stopping at a village inn there came up a thunderstorm, and Captain Hall, surprised that a new country should have reached such perfection in these meteorological manufactures, said to a bystander, "Why, you have very heavy thunder here." "Well, yes," replied the man, "we *du*, considerin' the number of inhabitants." Here is another story which a stage-driver told me once. A wag on the outside of the coach called to a man by the roadside who was fencing some very poor land: "I say, mister, what are you fencing that pasture for? It would take forty acres on 't to starve a middle-sized cow." "Jesso; and I 'm a-fencing of it to keep eour kettle cout."

Now in the "forty acre" part of this story we have an instance of what is called American exaggeration, and which I take to be the symptom of most promise in Yankee fun. For it marks that desire for intensity of expression which is one phase of imagination. Indeed many of these sayings are purely imaginative; as where a man said of a painter he knew, that "he painted a shingle so exactly like marble that when it fell into the river it sunk." A man told me once that the people of a certain town were so universally dishonest that "they had to take in their stone walls at night." In some of these stories imagination appears yet more strongly, and in that contradictory union with the understanding lies at the root of highest humor. For example, a coachman driving up some steep mountains in Vermont was asked if they were as steep on the other side also. "Steep! chain-lightnin' could n't go down 'em without the breechin' on." I believe that there is more latent humor among the American people than in any other, and that it will one day develop itself and find expression through Art.

If we apply the definitions we have made to Butler's poem, we shall find that it is not properly humorous at all; that the nearest approach to the humorous is burlesque. Irony is Butler's favorite weapon. But he always has an ulterior object. His characters do not live at all, but are only caricatured effigies of political enemies stuffed with bran and set up as targets for his wit. He never lets us forget for a moment that Presbyterian and Independent are primarily knaves and secondarily men. The personality never by accident expands into humanity. There is not a trace of imagination or of sympathy in his poem. It is pure satire, and intellectual satire only. There is as much creativeness in Trumbull's "McFingal," or Fessenden's "Terrible Tractoration" as in "Hudibras." Butler never works from within, but stands as a spectator covering his victims with merciless ridicule; and we enjoy the fun because his figures are as mere nobodies as Punch and Judy, whose misfortunes are meant to amuse us, and whose unreality is part of the sport. The characters of truly humorous writers are as real to us as any of our acquaintances. We no more doubt the existence of the Wife of Bath, of Don Quixote and Sancho, of Falstaff, Sir Roger de Coverley, Parson Adams, the Vicar, Uncle Toby, Pickwick or Major Pendennis, than we do our own. They are the contemporaries of every generation forever. They are our immortal friends whose epitaph no man shall ever write. The only incantation needed to summon them is the taking of a book from our shelf, and they are with us with their wisdom, their wit, their courtesy, their humanity, and (dearer than all) their weaknesses.

But the figures of Butler are wholly contemporaneous with himself. They are dead things nailed to his age, like crows to a barn-door, for an immediate *in terrorem* purpose, to waste and blow away with time and weather. The Guy Fawkes of a Fifth of November procession has as much manhood in it.

Butler, then, is a wit — in the strictest sense of the word — with only such far-off hints at humor as lie in a sense of the odd, the droll, or the ludicrous. But in wit he is supreme. "Hudibras" is as full of point as a paper of pins; it sparkles like a phosphorescent sea, every separate drop of which contains half a dozen little fiery lives. Indeed, the fault of the poem (if it can be called a fault) is that it has too much wit to be easy reading.

Butler had been a great reader, and out of the dryest books of school divinity, Puritan theology, metaphysics, medicine, astrology, mathematics, no matter what, his brain secreted wit as naturally as a field of corn will get so much silex out of a soil as would make flints for a whole arsenal of old-fashioned muskets, and where even Prometheus himself could not have found enough to strike a light with. I do sincerely believe that he would have found fun in a joke of Senator — well, any senator; and that is saying a great deal. I speak of course, of senators at Washington.

Mr. Lowell illustrated his criticism by copious quotations from "Hudibras." He concluded thus:

It would not be just to leave Butler without adding that he was an honest and apparently disinterested man. He wrote an indignant satire against the vices of Charles the Second's court. Andrew Marvel, the friend of Milton, and the pattern of incorruptible Republicanism, himself a finer poet and almost as great a wit as Butler — while he speaks contemptuously of the controversialists and satirists of his day, makes a special exception of "Hudibras." I can fancy John Bunyan enjoying it furtively, and Milton, if he had had such a thing as fun in him, would have laughed over it.

Many greater men and greater poets have left a less valuable legacy to their countrymen than Butler, who has made them the heirs of a perpetual fund of good humor, which is more nearly allied to good morals than most people suspect.

LECTURE IX

POPE

(Thursday Evening, February 6, 1855)

IX

THERE is nothing more curious, whether in the history of individual men or of nations, than the reactions which occur at more or less frequent intervals.

The human mind, both in persons and societies, is like a pendulum which, the moment it has reached the limit of its swing in one direction, goes inevitably back as far on the other side, and so on forever.

These reactions occur in everything, from the highest to the lowest, from religion to fashions of dress. The close crop and sober doublet of the Puritan were followed by the laces and periwigs of Charles the Second. The scarlet coats of our grandfathers have been displaced by as general a blackness as if the world had all gone into mourning. Tight sleeves alternate with loose, and the full-sailed expanses of Navarino have shrunk to those close-reefed phenomena which, like Milton's Demogorgon, are the *name* of bonnet without its appearance.

English literature, for half a century from the Restoration, showed the marks of both reaction and of a kind of artistic vassalage to France. From the compulsory saintship and short hair of the Roundheads the world rushed eagerly toward a little wickedness and a wilderness of wig. Charles the Second brought back with him French manners, French morals, and French taste. The fondness of the English for foreign fashions had long been noted. It was a favorite butt of the satirists of Elizabeth's day. Everybody remembers what *Portia* says of the English lord: "How oddly is he suited! I think he bought his doublet in Italy, his round hose in France, his bonnet in Germany, and his behavior everywhere."

Dryden is the first eminent English poet whose works show the marks of French influence, and a decline from the artistic toward the artificial, from nature toward fashion. Dryden had known Milton, had visited the grand old man probably in that "small chamber hung with rusty green," where he is described as "sitting in an elbow-chair, neatly dressed in black, pale but not cadaverous"; or had found him as he "used to sit in a gray, coarse cloth coat, at the door of his house near Bunhill Fields, in warm, sunny weather, to enjoy the fresh air." Dryden undertook to put the "Paradise Lost" into rhyme, and on Milton's leave being asked, he said, rather contemptuously, "Ay, he may *tag* my verses if he will." He also said that Dryden was a "good rhymist, but no poet." Dryden turned the great epic into a drama called "The State of Innocence," and intended for representation on the stage. Sir Walter Scott dryly remarks that the *costume* of our first parents made it rather an awkward thing to bring them before the footlights. It is an illustration of the character of the times that Dryden makes Eve the mouthpiece of something very like obscenity. Of the taste shown by such a travesty nothing need be said.

In the poems of Dryden nothing is more striking than the alternations between natural vigor and warmth of temperament and the merest commonplaces of diction. His strength lay chiefly in the understanding, and for weight of sterling sense and masculine English, and force of argument, I know nothing better than his prose. His mind was a fervid one, and I think that in his verse he sometimes mistook metrical enthusiasm for poetry. In his poems we find wit, fancy, an amplitude of nature, a rapid and graphic statement of the externals and antitheses of character, and a dignified fluency of verse rising sometimes to majesty — but not much imagination in the high poetic meaning of the term.

I have only spoken of his poems at all because they stand midway between the old era, which died with Milton and Sir Thomas Browne, and the new one which was just beginning. In the sixty years extending from 1660 to 1720, more French was imported into the language than at any other time since the Norman Conquest. What is of greater importance, it was French ideas and sentiments that were coming in now, and which shaped the spirit and, through that, the form of our literature.

The condition of the English mind at the beginning of the last century was one particularly capable of being magnetized from across the Channel. The loyalty of everybody, both in politics and religion, had been dislocated. A generation of materialists was to balance the over-spiritualism of the Puritans. The other world had had its turn long enough, and now *this* world was to have its chance. There seems to have been a universal skepticism, and in its most dangerous form — that is, united with a universal pretense of conformity. There was an unbelief that did not believe even in itself. Dean Swift, who looked forward to a bishopric, could write a book whose moral, if it had any, was that one religion was about as good as another, and accepted a cure of souls when it was doubtful if he thought men had any souls to be saved, or, at any rate, that they were worth saving if they had. The answer which Pulci's *Margutte* makes to *Morgante*, when he asks him if he believed in Christ or Mahomet, would have expressed well enough the creed of the majority of that generation:

> Margutte answered then, To tell thee truly,
>   My faith in black's no greater than in azure;
> But I believe in capons, roast meat, bouilli,
>   And above all in wine — and carnal pleasure.

It was impossible that anything truly great — great, I mean, on the moral and emotional as well as on the intellectual sides — could be produced in such a generation. But something intellectually great could be, and was. The French mind, always stronger in the perceptive and analytic than in the imaginative faculty, loving precision, grace, and fineness, had brought wit and fancy, and the elegant arts of society, to the perfection, almost, of science. Its ideal in literature was to combine the appearance of carelessness and gayety of thought with intellectual exactness of statement. Its influence, then, in English literature will appear chiefly in neatness and facility of expression, in point of epigrammatic compactness of phrase, and these in conveying conventional rather than universal experiences; in speaking for good society rather than for man.

Thus far in English poetry we have found life represented by Chaucer, the real life of men and women; the ideal or interior life as it relates to this world, by Spenser; what may be called imaginative life, by Shakspeare; the religious sentiment, or interior life as it relates to the other world, by Milton. But everything aspires toward a rhythmical utterance of itself, and accordingly the intellect and life, as it relates to what may be called the world, were waiting for their poet. They found or made a most apt one in Alexander Pope.

He stands for perfectness of intellectual expression, and it is a striking instance how much success and permanence of reputation depend upon conscientious and laborious finish as well as upon natural endowments.

I confess that I come to the treatment of Pope with diffidence. I was brought up in the old superstition that he was the greatest poet that ever lived, and when I came to find that I had instincts of my own, and my mind was brought in contact with the apostles of a more esoteric doctrine of poetry, I felt that ardent desire for smashing the idols I had been brought up to worship, without any regard to their artistic beauty, which characterizes youthful zeal.

What was it to me that Pope was a master of style? I felt, as Addison says in his "Freeholder" in answering an argument in favor of the Pretender because he could speak English and George I could not, "that I did not wish to be tyrannized over in the best English that was ever spoken." There was a time when I could not read Pope, but disliked him by instinct, as old Roger Ascham seems to have felt about Italy when he says: "I was once in Italy myself, but I thank God my abode there was only nine days."

But Pope fills a very important place in the history of English poetry, and must be studied by every one who would come to a clear knowledge of it. I have since read every line that Pope ever wrote, and every letter written by or to him, and that more than once. If I have not come to the conclusion that he is the greatest of poets, I believe I am at least in a condition to allow him every merit that is fairly his. I have said that Pope as a literary man represents precision and grace of expression; but, as a fact, he represents something more — nothing less, namely, than one of those external controversies of taste which will last as long as the Imagination and Understanding divide men between them. It is not a matter to be settled by any amount of argument or demonstration. Men are born Popists or Wordsworthians, Lockists or Kantists; and there is nothing more to be said of the matter. We do not hear that the green spectacles persuaded the horse into thinking that shavings were grass.

That reader is happiest whose mind is broad enough to enjoy the natural school for its nature and the artificial for its artificiality, provided they be only good of their kind. At any rate, we must allow that a man who can produce one perfect work is either a great genius or a very lucky one. As far as we who read are concerned, it is of secondary importance which. And Pope has done this in the "Rape of the Lock." For wit, fancy, invention, and keeping, it has never been surpassed. I do not say that there is in it poetry of the highest order, or that Pope is a poet whom any one would choose as the companion of his best hours. There is no inspiration in it, no trumpet call; but for pure entertainment it is unmatched.

The very earliest of Pope's productions gives indications of that sense and discretion, as well as wit, which afterwards so eminently distinguished him. The facility of expression is remarkable, and we find also that perfect balance of metre which he afterwards carried so far as to be wearisome. His pastorals were written in his sixteenth year, and their publication immediately brought him into notice. The following four verses from the first Pastoral are quite characteristic in their antithetic balance:

> You that, too wise for pride, too good for power,
> Enjoy the glory to be great no more,
> And carrying with you all the world can boast,
> To all the world illustriously are lost.

The sentiment is affected, and reminds one of that future period of Pope's correspondence with his friends, where Swift, his heart corroding with disappointed ambition at Dublin, Bolingbroke raising delusive turnips at his farm, and Pope pretending to disregard the lampoons which embittered his life, played together the solemn farce of affecting to despise the world which it would have agonized them to be forgotten by.

In Pope's next poem, the "Essay on Criticism," the wit and poet become apparent. It is full of clear thoughts compactly expressed. In this poem, written when Pope was only twenty-one, occur some of those lines which have become proverbial, such as:

> A little learning is a dangerous thing;
>
> For fools rush in where angels fear to tread;

> True Wit is Nature to advantage dressed,
> What oft was thought, but ne'er so well expressed;

> For each ill author is as bad a friend.

In all these we notice that terseness in which (regard being had to his especial range of thought) Pope has never been equaled. One cannot help being struck also with the singular *discretion* which the poem gives evidence of. I do not know where to look for another author in whom it appeared so early; and considering the vivacity of his mind and the constantly besetting temptation of his wit, it is still more wonderful. In his boyish correspondence with poor old Wycherly, one would suppose him to be a man and Wycherly the youth. Pope's understanding was no less vigorous than his fancy was lightsome and sprightly.

I come now to what in itself would be enough to have immortalized him as a poet, the "Rape of the Lock," in which, indeed, he appears more purely as a poet than in any other of his productions. Elsewhere he has shown more force, more wit, more reach of thought, but nowhere such a truly artistic combination of elegance and fancy. His genius has here found its true direction, and the very same artificiality which in his Pastorals was unpleasing heightens the effect and adds to the general keeping. As truly as Shakspeare is the poet of man as God made him, dealing with great passions and innate motives, so truly is Pope the poet of society, the delineator of manners, the exposer of those motives which may be called acquired, whose spring is in institutions and habits of purely worldly origin.

The whole poem more truly deserves the name of a creation than anything Pope ever wrote. The action is confined to a world of his own, the supernatural agency is wholly of his own contrivance, and nothing is allowed to overstep the limitations of the subject. It ranks by itself as one of the purest works of human fancy. Whether that fancy be truly poetical or not is another matter. The perfection of form in the "Rape of the Lock" is to me conclusive evidence that in it the natural genius of Pope found fuller and freer expression than in any other of his poems. The others are aggregates of brilliant passages rather than harmonious wholes.

Mr. Lowell gave a detailed analysis of the poem, with extracts of some length.

The "Essay on Man" has been praised and admired by men of the most opposite beliefs, and men of no belief at all. Bishops and free-thinkers have met here on a common ground of sympathetic approval. And, indeed, there is no particular faith in it. It is a droll medley of inconsistent opinions.

It proves only two things beyond a question: that Pope was not a great thinker; and that wherever he found a thought, no matter what, he would express it so tersely, so clearly, and with such smoothness of versification, as to give it an everlasting currency. Hobbes's unwieldy "Leviathan," left stranded on the shore of the last age and nauseous with the stench of its selfishness — from this Pope distilled a fragrant oil with which to fill the brilliant lamps of his philosophy, lamps like those in the tombs of alchemists, that go out the moment the healthy air is let in upon them. The only positive doctrine in the poem is the selfishness of Hobbes set to music, and the pantheism of Spinoza brought down from mysticism to commonplace. Nothing can be more absurd than many of the dogmas taught in the "Essay on Man."

The accuracy on which Pope prided himself, and for which he is commended, was not accuracy of thought so much as of expression. But the supposition is that in the "Essay on Man" Pope did not know what he was writing himself. He was only the condenser and epigrammatizer of Bolingbroke — a fitting St. John for such a gospel. Or if he *did* know, we can account for the contradictions by supposing that he threw in some of the commonplace moralities to conceal his real drift. Johnson asserts that Bolingbroke in private laughed at Pope's having been made the mouthpiece of opinions which he did not hold. But this is hardly probable when we consider the relations between them. It is giving Pope altogether too little credit for intelligence to suppose that he did not understand the principles of his intimate friend.

Dr. Warburton makes a rather lame attempt to ward off the charge of Spinozism from the "Essay on Man." He would have found it harder to show that the acknowledgment of any divine revelation would not overthrow the greater part of its teachings. If Pope intended by his poem all that the Bishop takes for granted in his commentary, we must deny him what is usually claimed as his first merit — clearness. If we did *not*, we grant him clearness as a writer at the expense of sincerity as a man. Perhaps a more charitable solution of the difficulty is that Pope's precision of thought was not equal to his polish of style.

But it is in his "Moral Essays" and part of his "Satires" that Pope deserves the praise which he himself desired —

> Happily to steer
> From grave to gay, from lively to severe.
> Correct with spirit, eloquent with ease,
> Intent to reason, or polite to please.

Here Pope must be allowed to have established a style of his own, in which he is without a rival. One can open upon wit and epigram at every page.

In his epistle on the characters of woman, no one who has ever known a noble woman will find much to please him. The climax of his praise rather degrades than elevates:

> O blest in temper, whose unclouded ray
> Can make to-morrow cheerful as to-day,
> She who can love a sister's charms, or hear
> Sighs for a daughter with unwounded ear,
> She who ne'er answers till a husband cools,
> Or if she rules him, never shows she rules,
> Charms by accepting, by submitting sways,
> Yet has her humor most when she obeys;
> Let fops or fortune fly which way they will,
> Disdains all loss of tickets, or codille,
> Spleen, vapors, or smallpox, above them all;
> And mistress of herself though china fall.

The last line is very witty and pointed; but consider what an ideal of womanly nobleness he must have had who praises his heroine for not being jealous of her daughter.

It is very possible that the women of Pope's time were as bad as they could be, but if God made poets for anything it was to keep alive the traditions of the pure, the holy, and the beautiful. I grant the influence of the age, but there is a sense in which the poet is of no age, and Beauty, driven from every other home, will never be an outcast and a wanderer while there is a poet-nature left; will never fail of the tribute at least of a song. It seems to me that Pope had a sense of the nice rather than of the beautiful. His nature delighted in the blemish more than in the charm.

Personally, we know more about Pope than about any of our poets. He kept no secret about himself. If he did not let the cat out of the bag, he always contrived to give her tail a pinch so that we might know she was there. In spite of the savageness of his satires, his disposition seems to have been a truly amiable one, and his character as an author was as purely fictitious as his style. I think that there was very little real malice in him.

A great deal must be allowed to Pope for the age in which he lived, and not a little, I think, for the influence of Swift. In his own province he still stands unapproachably alone. If to be the greatest satirist of individual men rather than of human nature; if to be the highest expression which the life of court and the ball-room has ever found in verse; if to have added more phrases to our language than any other but Shakspeare; if to have charmed four generations makes a man a great poet, then he is one. He was the chief founder of an artificial style of writing which in his hand was living and powerful because he used it to express artificial modes of thinking and an artificial state of society. Measured by any high standard of imagination, he will be found wanting; tried by any test of wit, he is unrivaled.

To what fatuities his theory of correctness led in the next generation, when practised upon by men who had not his genius, I shall endeavor to show in my next lecture.

LECTURE X

POETIC DICTION

(Friday Evening, February 9, 1855)

X

NO one who has read any early poems, of whatever nation, can have failed to notice a freshness in the language — a sort of game flavor, as it were — that gradually wastes out of it when poetry becomes domesticated, so to speak, and has grown to be a mere means of amusement both to writers and readers, instead of answering a deeper necessity in their natures. Our Northern ancestors symbolized the eternal newness of song by calling it the Present, and its delight by calling it the drink of Odin.

There was then a fierce democracy of words; no grades had then been established, and no favored ones advanced to the Upper House of Poetry. Men had a meaning, and so their words had to have one, too. They were not representatives of value, but value itself. They say that Valhalla was roofed with golden shields; that was what they believed, and in their songs they called them golden shingles. We should think shields the more poetical word of the two; but to them the poetry was in the *thing*, and the thought of it and the phrase took its life and meaning from them.

It is one result of the admixture of foreign words in our language that we use a great many phrases without knowing the force of them. There is a metaphoric vitality hidden in almost all of them, and we talk poetry as Molière's citizen did prose, without ever suspecting it. Formerly men *named* things; now we merely label them to know them apart. The Vikings called their ships sea-horses, just as the Arabs called their camels ships of the desert. Capes they called sea-noses, without thinking it an undignified term which the land would resent. And still, where mountains and headlands have the luck to be baptized by uncultivated persons, Fancy stands godmother. Old Greylock, up in Berkshire, got his surname before we had State geologists or distinguished statesmen. So did Great Haystack and Saddle-Mountain. Sailors give good names, if they have no dictionary aboard, and along our coasts, here and there, the word and the thing agree, and therefore are poetical. Meaning and poetry still cling to some of our common phrases, and the crow-foot, mouse-ear, goat's-beard, day's-eye, heart's-ease, snow-drop, and many more of their vulgar little fellow-citizens of the wood and roadsides are as happy as if Linnæus had never been born. Such names have a significance even to one who has never seen the things they stand for, but whose fancy would not be touched about a pelargonium unless he had an acquired sympathy with it. Our "cumulus" language, heaped together from all quarters, is like the clouds at sunset, and every man finds something different in a sentence, according to his associations. Indeed, every language that has become a literary one may be compared to a waning moon, out of which the light of beauty fades more and more. Only to poets and lovers does it repair itself from its luminous fountains.

The poetical quality of diction depends on the force and intensity of meaning with which it is employed. We are all of us full of latent significance, and let a poet have but the power to touch *us*, we forthwith enrich his word with ourselves, pouring into his verse our own lives, all our own experience, and take back again, without knowing it, the vitality which we had given away out of ourselves. Put passion enough into a word, and no matter what it is it becomes poetical; it is no longer what it was, but is a messenger from original man to original man, an ambassador from royal Thee to royal Me, and speaks to us from a level of equality. Pope, who did not scruple to employ the thoughts of Billingsgate, is very fastidious about the dress they come in, and claps a tawdry livery-coat on them, that they may be fit for the service of so fine a gentleman. He did not mind being coarse in idea, but it would have been torture to him to be thought commonplace. The sin of composition which he dreaded was,

> Lest ten low words should creep in one dull line.

But there is no more startling proof of the genius of Shakspeare than that he always lifts the language up to himself, and never thinks to raise himself atop of it. If he has need of the service of what is called a low word, he takes it, and it is remarkable how many of his images are borrowed out of the street and the workshop. His pen ennobled them all, and we feel as if they had been knighted for good service in the field. Shakspeare, as we all know (for does not Mr. Voltaire say so?), was a vulgar kind of fellow, but somehow or other his genius will carry the humblest things up into the air of heaven as easily as Jove's eagle bore Ganymede.

Whatever is used with a great meaning, and conveys that meaning to others in its full intensity, is no longer common and ordinary. It is this which gives their poetic force to symbols, no matter how low their origin. The blacksmith's apron, once made the royal standard of Persia, can fill armies with enthusiasm and is as good as the oriflamme of France. A broom is no very noble thing in itself, but at the mast-head of a brave old De Ruyter, or in the hands of that awful shape which Dion the Syracusan saw, it becomes poetical. And so the emblems of the tradesmen of Antwerp, which they bore upon their standards, pass entirely out of the prosaic and mechanical by being associated with feelings and deeds that were great and momentous.

Mr. Lowell here read a poem by Dr. Donne entitled "The Separation."

As respects Diction, *that* becomes formal and technical when poetry has come to be considered an artifice rather than an art, and when its sole object is to revive certain pleasurable feelings already conventional, instead of originating new sources of delight. Then it is truly earth to earth; dead language used to bury dead emotion in. This kind of thing was carried so far by the later Scandinavian poets that they compiled a dictionary of the metaphors used by the elder Skalds (whose songs were the utterance of that within them which *would* be spoken), and satisfied themselves with a new arrangement of them. Inspiration was taught, as we see French advertised to be, in six lessons.

In narrative and descriptive poetry we feel that proper keeping demands a certain choice and luxury of words. The question of propriety becomes one of prime importance here. Certain terms have an acquired imaginative value from the associations they awake in us. Certain words are more musical than others. Some rhymes are displeasing; some measures wearisome. Moreover, there are words which have become indissolubly entangled with ludicrous or mean ideas. Hence it follows that there is such a thing as Poetic Diction, and it was this that Milton was thinking of when he spoke of making our English "search her coffers round."

I will illustrate this. Longfellow's "Evangeline" opens with a noble solemnity:

This is the forest primeval; the murmuring pines and the hemlocks,
Bearded with moss and in garments green, indistinct in the twilight,
Stand like the Druids of eld, with voices sad and prophetic,
Stand like harpers hoar, with beards that rest on their bosoms.
Loud from its rocky caverns the deep-voiced neighboring ocean
Speaks, and in accents disconsolate answers the wail of the forest.

POETIC DICTION

There is true feeling here, and the sigh of the pines is heard in the verses. I can find only one epithet to hang a criticism on, and that is the "*wail of the forest*" in the last line, which is not in keeping with the general murmur. Now I do not suppose that the poet turned over any vocabulary to find the words he wanted, but followed his own poetic instinct altogether in the affair. But suppose for a moment, that instead of being a true poet, he had been only a gentleman versifying; suppose he had written, "This is the primitive forest." The prose meaning is the same, but the poetical meaning, the music, and the cadence would be gone out of it, and gone forever. Or suppose that, instead of "garments green," he had said "dresses green"; the idea is identical, but the phrase would have come down from its appropriate remoteness to the milliner's counter. But not to take such extreme instances, only substitute instead of "harpers hoar," the words "harpers gray," and you lose not only the alliteration, but the fine hoarse sigh of the original epithet, which blends with it the general feeling of the passage. So if you put "sandy beaches" in the place of "rocky caverns," you will not mar the absolute truth to nature, but you will have forfeited the relative truth to keeping.

When Bryant says so exquisitely,

> Painted moths
> Have *wandered the blue sky* and died again,

we ruin the poetry, the sunny spaciousness of the image, without altering the prose sense, by substituting

> Have *flown through the clear air.*

But the words "poetic diction" have acquired a double meaning, or perhaps I should say there are two kinds of poetic diction, the one true and the other false, the one real and vital, the other mechanical and artificial. Wordsworth for a time confounded the two together in one wrathful condemnation, and preached a crusade against them both. He wrote, at one time, on the theory that the language of ordinary life was the true dialect of poetry, and that one word was as good as another. He seemed even to go farther and to adopt the Irishman's notion of popular equality, that "one man is as good as another, and a dale better, too." He preferred, now and then, prosaic words and images to poetical ones. But he was not long in finding his mistake and correcting it. One of his most tender and pathetic poems, "We are Seven," began thus in the first edition:

A simple child, *dear brother Jim.*

All England laughed, and in the third edition Wordsworth gave in and left the last half of the line blank, as it has been ever since. If the poem had been a translation from the Turkish and had begun,

A simple child, dear Ibrahim,

there would have been nothing unpoetical in it; but the "dear brother Jim," which would seem natural enough at the beginning of a familiar letter, is felt to be ludicrously incongruous at the opening of a poem.

To express a profound emotion, the simpler the language and the less removed from the ordinary course of life the better. There is a very striking example of this in Webster's tragedy of "The Duchess of Malfy." The brother of the Duchess has procured her murder, and when he comes in and sees the body he merely says:

"Cover her face; mine eyes dazzle; she died young."

Horror could not be better expressed than in these few words, and Webster has even taken care to break up the verse in such a way that a too entire consciousness of the metre may not thrust itself between us and the bare emotion he intends to convey.

In illustration, Mr. Lowell quoted from Shakspeare ("Henry V"), Marlowe, Chapman, Dunbar, Beaumont and Fletcher, Waller, Young, and Cawthorn.

These men [the poets of the eighteenth century] were perfectly conscious of the fact that poetry is not produced under an ordinary condition of the mind, and accordingly, when they begin to grind their barrel-organs, they go through the ceremony of invoking the Muse, talk in the blandest way of divine rages and sacred flames, and one thing or another, and ask for holy fire to heat their little tea-urns with as coolly as one would borrow a lucifer. They appeal ceremoniously to the "sacred Nine," when the only thing really necessary to them was the ability to count as high as the sacred ten syllables that constituted their verse. If the Muse had once granted their prayer, if she *had* once unveiled her awful front to the poor fellows, they would have hidden under their beds, every man John of them.

The eighteenth century produced some true poets, but almost all, even of them, were infected by the prevailing style. I cannot find any name that expresses it better than the "Dick Swiveller style." As Dick always called wine the "rosy," sleep the "balmy," and so forth, so did these perfectly *correct* gentlemen always employ either a fluent epithet or a diffuse paraphrasis to express the commonest emotions or ideas. If they wished to say *tea* they would have done it thus:

> Of China's herb the infusion hot and mild.

Coffee would be

> The fragrant juice of Mocha's kernel gray,

or brown or black, as the rhyme demanded. A boot is dignified into

> The shining leather that the leg encased.

Wine is

> The purple honor of th' ambrosial vine.

All women are "nymphs," carriages are "harnessed pomps," houses are sumptuous or humble "piles," as the case may be, and everything is purely technical. Of nature there seems to have been hardly a tradition.

But instead of attempting to describe in prose the

diluent diction which passed for poetic under the artificial system — which the influence of Wordsworth did more than anything else to abolish and destroy — I will do it by a few verses in the same style. Any subject will do — a Lapland sketch, we will say:

> Where far-off suns their fainter splendors throw
> O'er Lapland's wastes of uncongenial snow,
> Where giant icebergs lift their horrent spires
> And the blank scene a gelid fear expires.
> Where oft the aurora of the northern night
> Cheats with pale beams of ineffectual light,
> Where icy Winter broods o'er hill and plain,
> And Summer never comes, or comes in vain;
> Yet here, e'en here, kind Nature grants to man
> A boon congenial with her general plan.
> Though no fair blooms to vernal gales expand,
> And smiling Ceres shuns th' unyielding land,
> Behold, even here, cast up a monstrous spoil,
> The sea's vast monarch yields nutritious oil,
> Escaped, perchance, from where the unfeeling crews
> Dart the swift steel, and hempen coils unloose,
> He whirls impetuous through the crimson tide,
> Nor heeds the death that quivers in his side;
> Northward he rushes with impulsive fin,
> Where shores of crystal groan with ocean's din,
> Shores that will melt with pity's glow more soon
> Than the hard heart that launched the fierce harpoon.

POETIC DICTION

In vain! he dies! yet not without avail
The blubbery bulk between his nose and tail.
Soon shall that bulk, in liquid amber stored,
Shed smiling plenty round some Lapland board.
Dream not, ye nymphs that flutter round the tray
When suns declining shut the door of day,
While China's herb, infused with art, ye sip,
And toast and scandal share the eager lip.
Dream not to you alone that Life is kind,
Nor Hyson's charms alone can soothe the mind;
If you are blest, ah, how more blest is he
By kinder fate shut far from tears and tea,
Who marks, replenished by his duteous hand.
Dark faces oleaginously expand;
And while you faint to see the scalding doom
Invade with stains the pride of Persia's loom,
Happier in skins than you in silks perhaps,
Deals the bright train-oil to his little Lap's.

LECTURE XI

WORDSWORTH

(Tuesday Evening, February 13, 1855)

XI

A FEW remarks upon two of the more distinguished poets of the eighteenth century will be a fitting introduction to Wordsworth, and, indeed, a kind of commentary on his poetry. Of two of these poets we find very evident traces in him — Thomson and Cowper — of the one in an indiscriminating love of nature, of the other in a kind of domestic purity, and of both in the habit of treating subjects essentially prosaic, in verse; whence a somewhat swelling wordiness is inevitable.

Thomson had the good luck to be born in Scotland, and to be brought up by parents remarkable for simplicity and piety of life. Living in the country till he was nearly twenty, he learned to love natural beauty, and must have been an attentive student of scenery. That he had true instincts in poetry is proved by his making Milton and Spenser his models. He was a man of force and originality, and English poetry owes him a large debt as the first who stood out both in precept and practice against the vicious artificial style which then reigned, and led the way back to purer tastes and deeper principles. He was a man perfectly pure in life; the associate of eminent and titled personages, without being ashamed of the little milliner's shop of his sisters in Edinburgh; a lover of freedom, and a poet who never lost a friend, nor ever wrote a line of which he could repent. The licentiousness of the age could not stain him. His poem of "Winter" was published a year before the appearance of the "Dunciad."

Thomson's style is not equal to his conceptions. It is generally lumbering and diffuse, and rather stilted than lofty. It is very likely that his Scotch birth had something to do with this, and that he could not write English with that unconsciousness without which elegance is out of the question — for there can be no true elegance without freedom. Burns's English letters and poems are examples of this.

But there are passages in Thomson's poems full of the truest feelings for nature, and gleams of pure imagination.

Mr. Lowell here read a passage from "Summer," which, he said, illustrated better than almost any other his excellences and defects. It is a description of a storm, beginning:

> At first heard solemn o'er the verge of Heaven
> The tempest growls.

This is fustian patched with cloth of gold. The picture, fine as it is in parts, is too much frittered with particulars. The poet's imagination does not seem powerful enough to control the language. There is no autocratic energy, but the sentences are like unruly barons, each doing what he likes in his own province. Many of them are prosaic and thoroughly *un*picturesque, and come under the fatal condemnation of being *flat*. Yet throughout the passage,

> The unconquerable genius struggles through

half-suffocated in a cloud of words.

But the metre is hitchy and broken, and seems to have no law but that of five feet to the verse. There is no Pegasean soar, but the unwieldy gallop of an ox. The imagination, which Thomson undoubtedly had, contrasted oddly with the lumbering vehicle of his diction. He takes a bushel-basket to bring home an egg in. In him poetry and prose entered into partnership, and poetry was the sleeping partner who comes down now and then to see how the business is getting on. But he had the *soul* of a poet, and that is the main thing.

Of Gray and Collins there is no occasion to speak at length in this place. Both of them showed true poetic imagination. In Gray it was thwarted by an intellectual timidity that looked round continually for precedent; and Collins did not live long enough to discharge his mind thoroughly of classic pedantry; but both of them broke away from the reigning style of decorous frigidity. Collins's "Ode to Evening" is enough to show that he had a sincere love of nature — but generally the scenery of both is borrowed from books.

In Cowper we find the same over-minuteness in describing which makes Thomson wearisome, but relieved by a constant vivacity of fancy which in Thomson was entirely wanting. But Cowper more distinctly preluded Wordsworth in his delight in simple things, in finding themes for his song in the little incidents of his own fireside life, or his daily walks, and especially in his desire to make poetry a means of conveying moral truth. The influence of Cowper may be traced clearly in some of Wordsworth's minor poems of pure fancy, and there is one poem of his — that on "Yardly Oak" — which is almost perfectly Wordsworthian. But Cowper rarely rises above the region of fancy, and he often applied verse to themes that would not sing. His poetry is never more than agreeable, and never reaches down to the deeper sources of delight. Cowper was one of those men who, wanting a vigorous understanding to steady the emotional part of his nature, may be called peculiar rather than original. Great poetry can never be made out of a morbid temperament, and great wits are commonly the farthest removed from madness. But Cowper had at least the power of believing that his own thoughts and pleasures were as good, and as fit for poetry, as those of any man, no matter how long he had enjoyed the merit of being dead.

The closing years of the eighteenth century have something in common with those of the sixteenth. The air was sparkling with moral and intellectual stimulus. The tremble of the French Revolution ran through all Europe, and probably England, since the time of the great Puritan revolt, had never felt such a thrill of national and indigenous sentiment as during the Napoleonic wars. It was a time fitted to give birth to something original in literature. If from the collision of minds sparks of wit and fancy fly out, the shock and jostle of great events, of world-shaping ideas, and of nations who do their work without knowing it, strike forth a fire that kindles heart and brain and tongue to more inspired conceptions and utterances.

It was fortunate for Wordsworth that he had his breeding in the country, and not only so, but among the grandest scenery of England. His earliest associates were the mountains, lakes, and streams of his native district, and the scenery with which his mind was stored during its most impressionable period was noble and pure. The people, also, among whom he grew up were a simple and hardy race, who kept alive the traditions and many of the habits of a more picturesque time. There was also a general equality of condition which kept life from becoming conventional and trite, and which cherished friendly human sympathies. When death knocked at any door of the hamlet, there was an echo from every fireside; and a wedding dropped an orange blossom at every door. There was not a grave in the little churchyard but had its story; not a crag or glen or aged tree without its legend. The occupations of the people, who were mostly small farmers and shepherds, were such as fostered independence and originality of character. And where everybody knew everybody, and everybody's father had known everybody's father, and so on immemorially, the interest of man in man was not likely to become a matter of cold hearsay and distant report. It was here that Wordsworth learned not only to love the simplicity of nature, but likewise that homely and earnest manliness which gives such depth and sincerity to his poems. Travel, intercourse with society, scholarly culture, nothing could cover up or obliterate those early impressions. They widened with the range of his knowledge and added to his power of expression, but they never blunted that fine instinct in him which enables him always to speak directly to men and to gentleman, or scholar, or citizen. It was this that enabled his poetry afterwards to conquer all the reviews of England. The great art of being a man, the sublime mystery of being *yourself*, is something to which one must be apprenticed early.

Mr. Lowell here gave an outline of Wordsworth's personal history and character.

As a man we fancy him just in the least degree uninteresting — if the horrid word must come out — why, a little bit of a bore. One must regard him as a prophet in order to have the right kind of feeling toward him; and prophets are excellent for certain moods of mind, but perhaps are creatures

>Too bright and good
>For human nature's daily food.

I fancy from what I have heard from those who knew him that he had a tremendous prose-power, and that, with his singing-robes off, he was dry and stiff as a figure-head. He had a purity of mind approaching almost to prudery, and a pupil of Dr. Arnold told me he had heard him say once at dinner that he thought the first line of Keats's ode to a "Grecian Urn" indecorous. The boys considered him rather *slow*. There was something rocky and unyielding in his mind; something that, if we found it in a man we did not feel grateful to and respect, we should call hard. Even his fancy sometimes is glittering and stiff, like crystallizations in granite. But at other times how tender and delicate and dewy from very contrast, like harebells growing in a crag-cleft!

There seem to have been two distinct natures in him — Wordsworth the poet, and Wordsworth the man who used to talk about Wordsworth the poet. One played a kind of Baruch to the other's Jeremiah, and thought a great deal of his master the prophet. Baruch was terrifically *un*inspired, and was in the habit of repeating Jeremiah's poems at rather more length than was desired, selecting commonly the parts which pleased him, Baruch, the best. Baruch Wordsworth used to praise Jeremiah Wordsworth, and used to tell entertaining anecdotes of him,—

how he one day saw an old woman and the next did *not*, and so came home and dictated some verses on this remarkable phenomenon; and how another day he saw a cow.

But in reading Wordsworth we must skip all the Baruch interpolations, and cleave wholly to Jeremiah, who is truly inspired and noble — more so than any modern. We are too near him, perhaps, to be able wholly to separate the personal from the poetical. I acknowledge that I reverence the noble old man both for his grand life and his poems, that are worthy expressions of it. But a lecturer is under bonds to speak what he believes to be the truth. While I think that Wordsworth's poetry is a thing by itself, both in its heights and depths, something sacred and apart, I cannot but acknowledge that his prosing is sometimes a gift as peculiar to himself. Like old Ben Jonson, he apparently wished that a great deal of what he wrote should be called "works." Especially is this true of his larger poems, like the "Excursion" and the "Prelude." However small, however commonplace the thought, the ponderous machine of his verse runs on like a railway train that must start at a certain hour though the only passenger be the boy that cries lozenges. He seems to have thought that inspiration was something that could be turned on like steam. Walter Savage Landor told me that he once said to Wordsworth: "Mr. Wordsworth, a man may mix as much poetry with prose as he likes, and it will make it the better; but the moment he mixes a bit of prose with his poetry, it precipitates the whole." Wordsworth, he added, never forgave him.

There was a great deal in Wordsworth's character that reminds us of Milton; the same self-reliance, the same purity and loftiness of purpose, and, I suspect, the same personal dryness of temperament and seclusion of self. He seems to have had a profounder imagination than Milton, but infinitely less music, less poetical faculty. I am not entirely satisfied of the truth of the modern philosophy which, if a man knocks another on the head, transfers all the guilt to some peccant bump on his own occiput or sinciput; but if we measure Wordsworth in this way, I feel as if he had plenty of forehead, but that he wanted hind-head, and would have been more entirely satisfactory if he had had one of the philo-something-or-other.

It cannot be denied that in Wordsworth the very highest powers of the poetical mind were associated with a certain tendency to the diffuse and commonplace. It is in the Understanding (always prosaic) that the great golden veins of his imagination are embedded. He wrote too much to write always well; for it is not a great Xerxes army of words, but a compact Greek ten thousand that march safely down to posterity. He sets tasks to the divine faculty, which is much the same as trying to make Jove's eagle do the service of a clucking hen. Throughout the "Prelude" and the "Excursion," he seems striving to bind the wizard imagination with the sand-ropes of dry disquisition, and to have forgotten the potent spell-word which would make the particulars adhere. There is an arenaceous quality in the style which makes progress wearisome; yet with what splendors of mountain-sunsets are we not rewarded! What golden rounds of verse do we not see stretching heavenward, with angels ascending and descending! What haunting melodies hover around us, deep and eternal, like the undying barytone of the sea! And if we are compelled to fare through sands and desert wilderness, how often do we not hear airy shapes that syllable our names with a startling personal appeal to our highest consciousness and our noblest aspiration, such as we might wait for in vain in any other poet.

Take from Wordsworth all which an honest criticism cannot but allow, and what is left will show how truly great he was. He had no humor, no dramatic power, and his temperament was of that dry and juiceless quality that in all his published correspondence you shall not find a letter, but only essays. If we consider carefully where he was most successful, we shall find that it was not so much in description of natural scenery, or delineation of character, as in vivid expression of the effect produced by external objects and events upon his own mind. His finest passages are always monologues. He had a fondness for particulars, and there are parts of his poems which remind us of local histories in the undue importance given to trivial matter. He was the historian of Wordsworthshire. This power of particularization (for it is as truly a power as generalization) is what gives such vigor and greatness to single lines and sentiments of Wordsworth, and to poems developing a single thought or word. It was this that made him so fond of the sonnet. His mind had not that reach and elemental movement of Milton's which, like the trade-winds, gathered to itself thoughts and images like stately fleets from every quarter; some, deep with silks and spicery, come brooding over the silent thunders of their battailous armaments, but all swept forward in their destined track, over the long billows of his verse, every inch of canvas strained by the unifying breath of their common epic impulse. It was an organ that Milton mastered, mighty in compass, capable equally of the trumpet's ardors, or the slim delicacy of the flute; and sometimes it bursts forth in great crashes through his prose, as if he touched it for solace in the intervals of his toil. If Wordsworth sometimes puts the trumpet to his lips, yet he lays it aside soon and willingly for his appropriate instrument, the pastoral reed. And it is not one that grew by any vulgar stream, but that which Apollo breathed through tending the flocks of Admetus, that which Pan endowed with every melody of the visible universe, the same in which the soul of the despairing nymph took refuge and gifted with her dual nature, so that ever and anon, amid notes of human joy and sorrow, there comes suddenly a deeper and almost awful tone, thrilling us into dim consciousness of a forgotten divinity.

Of no other poet, except Shakspeare, have so many phrases become household words as of Wordsworth. If Pope has made current more epigrams of worldly wisdom, to Wordsworth belongs the nobler praise of having defined for us, and given us for a daily possession, those faint and vague suggestions of other-worldliness of whose gentler ministry with our baser nature the hurry and bustle of life scarcely ever allowed us to be conscious. He has won for himself a secure immortality by a depth of intuition which makes only the best minds at their best hours worthy, or indeed capable, of his companionship, and by a homely sincerity of human sympathy which reaches the humblest heart. Our language owes him gratitude for the purity and abstinence of his style, and we who speak it, for having emboldened us to trust ourselves to take delight in simple things, and to trust ourselves to our own instincts. And he hath his reward. It needs not to

> Bid Beaumont lie
> A little farther off to make him room.

for there is no fear of crowding in that little society with whom he is now enrolled as the fifth in the succession of the great English poets.

LECTURE XII

THE FUNCTION OF THE POET

(Friday Evening, February 16, 1855*)*

XII

WHETHER, as some philosophers here assume, we possess only the fragments of a great cycle of knowledge, in whose center stood the primeval man in friendly relation with the powers of the universe, and build our hovels out of the ruins of our ancestral palace; or whether, according to the developing theory of others, we are rising gradually and have come up from an atom instead of descending from an Adam, so that the proudest pedigree might run up to a barnacle or a zoöphyte at last, are questions which will keep for a good many centuries yet. Confining myself to what little we can learn from History, we find tribes rising slowly out of barbarism to a higher or lower point of culture and civility, and everywhere the poet also is found under one name or another, changing in certain outward respects, but essentially the same.

But however far we go back, we shall find this also — that the poet and the priest were united originally in the same person: which means that the poet was he who was conscious of the world of spirit as well as that of sense, and was the ambassador of the gods to men. This was his highest function, and hence his name of seer.

I suppose the word *epic* originally meant nothing more than this, that the poet was the person who was the greatest master of speech. His were the ἔπεα πτερόεντα, the true winged words that could fly down the unexplored future and carry thither the names of ancestral heroes, of the brave, and wise, and good. It was thus that the poet could reward virtue, and, by and by, as society grew more complex, could burn in the brand of shame. This is Homer's character of Demodocus in the eighth book of the "Odyssey,"

> When the Muse loved and gave the good and ill,

the gift of conferring good or evil immortality.

The first histories were in verse, and, sung as they were at the feasts and gatherings of the people, they awoke in men the desire of fame, which is the first promoter of courage and self-trust, because it teaches men by degrees to appeal from the present to the future. We may fancy what the influence of the early epics was when they were recited to men who claimed the heroes celebrated in them for their ancestors, by what Bouchardon, the sculptor, said only two centuries ago: "When I read Homer I feel as if I were twenty feet high."

Nor have poets lost their power over the future in modern times. Dante lifts up by the hair the face of some petty traitor, the Smith and Brown of some provincial Italian town, lets the fire of his Inferno glare upon it for a moment, and it is printed forever on the memory of mankind. The historians may iron out the shoulders of Richard III. as smooth as they can; they will never get over the wrench that Shakspeare gave them.

The peculiarity of almost all early literature is that it seems to have a double meaning; that underneath its natural we find ourselves continually seeing and suspecting a supernatural meaning. Even in the older epics the characters seem to be only half-historical and half-typical. They appear as the Pilgrim Fathers do in Twenty-second of December speeches at Plymouth. The names may be historical, but the attributes are ideal. The orator draws a portrait rather of what he thinks the founders ought to have been than a likeness which contemporaries would have recognized. Thus did early poets endeavor to make reality out of appearances. For, except a few typical men in whom certain ideas get embodied, the generations of mankind are mere apparitions who come out of the dark for a purposeless moment, and enter the dark again after they have performed the nothing they came for.

The poet's gift, then, is that of seer. He it is that discovers the truth as it exists in types and images; that is the spiritual meaning, which abides forever under the sensual. And his instinct is to express himself also in types and images. But it was not only necessary that he himself should be delighted with his vision, but that he should interest his hearers with the faculty divine. Pure truth is not acceptable to the mental palate. It must be diluted with character and incident; it must be humanized in order to be attractive. If the bones of a mastodon be exhumed, a crowd will gather out of curiosity; but let the skeleton of a man be turned up, and what a difference in the expression of the features! Every bystander then creates his little drama, in which those whitened bones take flesh upon them and stalk as chief actor.

The poet is he who can best see or best say what is ideal; what belongs to the world of soul and of beauty. Whether he celebrates the brave and good, or the gods, or the beautiful as it appears in man or nature, something of a religious character still clings to him. He may be unconscious of his mission; he may be false to it, but in proportion as he is a great poet, he rises to the level of it more often. He does not always directly rebuke what is bad or base, but indirectly, by making us feel what delight there is in the good and fair. If he besiege evil it is with such beautiful engines of war (as Plutarch tells us of Demetrius) that the besieged themselves are charmed with them. Whoever reads the great poets cannot but be made better by it, for they always introduce him to a higher society, to a greater style of manners and of thinking. Whoever learns to love what is beautiful is made incapable of the mean and low and bad. It is something to be thought of, that all the great poets have been good men. He who translates the divine into the vulgar, the spiritual into the sensual, is the reverse of a poet.

It seems to be thought that we have come upon the earth too late; that there has been a feast of the imagination formerly, and all that is left for us is to steal the scraps. We hear that there is no poetry in railroads, steamboats, and telegraphs, and especially in Brother Jonathan. If this be true, so much the worse for him. But, because *he* is a materialist, shall there be no poets? When we have said that we live in a materialistic age, we have said something which meant more than we intended. If we say it in the way of blame, we have said a foolish thing, for probably one age is as good as another; and, at any rate, the worst is good enough company for us. The age of Shakspeare seems richer than our own only because he was lucky enough to have such a pair of eyes as his to see it and such a gift as his to report it. Shakspeare did not sit down and cry for the water of Helicon to turn the wheels of his little private mill there at the Bankside. He appears to have gone more quietly about his business than any playwright in London; to have drawn off what water-power he wanted from the great prosy current of affairs that flows alike for all, and in spite of all; to have ground for the public what grist they want, coarse or fine; and it seems a mere piece of luck that the smooth stream of his activity reflected with ravishing clearness every changing mood of heaven and earth, every stick and stone, every dog and clown and courtier that stood upon its brink. It is a curious illustration of the friendly manner in which Shakspeare received everything that came along, of what a *present* man he was, that in the very same year that the mulberry tree was brought into England, he got one and planted it in his garden at Stratford.

It is perfectly true that this is a materialistic age, and for this very reason we want our poets all the more. We find that every generation contrives to catch its singing larks without the sky's falling. When the poet comes he always turns out to be the man who discovers that the passing moment is the inspired one, and that the secret of poetry is not to have lived in Homer's day or Dante's, but to be alive now. To be alive now, that is the great art and mystery. They are dead men who live in the past, and men yet unborn who live in the future. We are like Hans-in-Luck, forever exchanging the burthensome good we have for something else, till at last we come home empty-handed. The people who find their own age prosaic are those who see only its costume. And this is what makes it prosaic: that we have not faith enough in ourselves to think that our own clothes are good enough to be presented to Posterity in. The artists seem to think that the court dress of posterity is that of Vandyke's time or Caesar's. I have seen the model of a statue of Sir Robert Peel — a statesman whose merit consisted in yielding gracefully to the present — in which the sculptor had done his best to travesty the real man into a make-believe Roman. At the period when England produced its greatest poets, we find exactly the reverse of this, and we are thankful to the man who made the monument of Lord Bacon that he had genius enough to copy every button of his dress, everything down to the rosettes on his shoes. These men had faith even in their own shoe-strings. Till Dante's time the Italian poets thought no language good enough to put their nothings into but Latin (and, indeed, a dead tongue was the best for dead thoughts), but Dante found the common speech of Florence, in which men bargained, and scolded, and made love, good enough for him, and out of the world around him made such a poem as no Roman ever sang.

We cannot get rid of our wonder, we who have brought down the wild lightning from writing fiery doom upon the walls of heaven to be our errand-boy and penny postman. In this day of newspapers and electric telegraphs, in which common-sense and ridicule can magnetise a whole continent between dinner and tea, we may say that such a phenomenon as Mahomet were impossible; and behold Joe Smith and the State of Deseret! Turning over the yellow leaves of the same copy of Webster on "Witchcraft" which Cotton Mather studied, I thought, Well, that goblin is laid at last! And while I mused, the tables were dancing and the chairs beating the devil's tattoo all over Christendom. I have a neighbor who dug down through tough strata of clay-slate to a spring pointed out by a witch-hazel rod in the hands of a seventh son's seventh son, and the water is sweeter to him for the wonder that is mixed with it. After all, it seems that our scientific gas, be it never so brilliant, is not equal to the dingy old Aladdin's lamp.

It is impossible for men to live in the world without poetry of some sort or another. If they cannot get the best, they will get at some substitute for it. But there is as much poetry as ever in the world if we can ever know how to find it out; and as much imagination, perhaps, only that it takes a more prosaic direction. Every man who meets with misfortune, who is stripped of his material prosperity, finds that he has a little outlying mountain-farm of imagination, which does not appear in the schedule of his effects, on which his spirit is able to keep alive, though he never thought of it while he was fortunate. Job turns out to be a great poet as soon as his flocks and herds are taken away from him.

Perhaps our continent will begin to sing by and by, as the others have done. We have had the Practical forced upon us by our condition. We have had a whole hemisphere to clear up and put to rights. And we are descended from men who were hardened and stiffened by a downright wrestle with Necessity. There was no chance for poetry among the Puritans. And yet if any people have a right to imagination, it should be the descendants of those very Puritans. They had enough of it, or they could not have conceived the great epic they did, whose books are States, and which is written on this continent from Maine to California.

John Quincy Adams, making a speech at New Bedford many years ago, reckoned the number of whale ships (if I remember rightly) that sailed out of that port, and, comparing it with some former period, took it as a type of American success. But, alas! it is with quite other oil that those far-shining lamps of a nation's true glory which burn forever must be filled. It is not by any amount of material splendor or prosperity, but only by moral greatness, by ideas, by works of the imagination, that a race can conquer the future. No voice comes to us from the once mighty Assyria but the hoot of the owl that nests amid her crumbling palaces; of Carthage, whose merchant fleets once furled their sails in every port of the known world, nothing is left but the deeds of Hannibal. She lies dead on the shore of her once subject sea, and the wind of the desert flings its handfuls of burial-sand upon her corpse. A fog can blot Holland or Switzerland out of existence. But how large is the space occupied in the maps of the soul by little Athens or powerless Italy. They were great by the soul, and their vital force is as indestructible as the soul.

Till America has learned to love Art, not as an

amusement, not as a mere ornament of her cities, not as a superstition of what is *comme il faut* for a great nation, but for its harmonizing and ennobling energy, for its power of making men better by arousing in them the perception of their own instincts for what is beautiful and sacred and religious, and an eternal rebuke of the base and worldly, she will not have succeeded in that high sense which alone makes a nation out of a people, and raises it from a dead name to a living power. Were our little mother-island sunk beneath the sea; or worse, were she conquered by Scythian barbarians, yet Shakspeare would be an immortal England, and would conquer countries when the bones of her last sailor had kept their ghastly watch for ages in unhallowed ooze beside the quenched thunders of her navy.

This lesson I learn from the past: that grace and goodness, the fair, the noble, and the true will never cease out of the world till the God from whom they emanate ceases out of it; that the sacred duty and noble office of the poet is to reveal and justify them to man; that as long as the soul endures, endures also the theme of new and unexampled song; that while there is grace in grace, love in love, and beauty in beauty, God will still send poets to find them, and bear witness of them, and to hang their ideal portraitures in the gallery of memory. *God with us* is forever the mystical theme of the hour that is passing. The lives of the great poets teach us that they were men of their generation who felt most deeply the meaning of the Present.

I have been more painfully conscious than any one else could be of the inadequacy of what I have been able to say, when compared to the richness and variety of my theme. I shall endeavor to make my apology in verse, and will bid you farewell in a little poem in which I have endeavored to express the futility of all *effort* to speak the loveliness of things, and also my theory of where the Muse is to be found, if ever. It is to her that I sing my hymn.

Mr. Lowell here read an original poem of considerable length, which concluded the lecture, and was received with bursts of applause.

www.ingramcontent.com/pod-product-compliance
Lightning Source LLC
Chambersburg PA
CBHW021843230426
43669CB00008B/1059